The
FOCALGUIDE
to the
Darkroo

THE (f) FOCALGUIDES TO

	Basic Photography
COLOUR	David Lynch
EFFECTS AND TRICKS	Günter Spitzing
EXPOSURE	David Lynch
LIGHTING	Paul Petzold
LOW LIGHT PHOTOGRAPHY	Paul Petzold
	Equipment
CAMERAS	Clyde Reynolds
FILTERS	Clyde Reynolds
FLASH	Günter Spitzing
LENSES	Leonard Gaunt
35 mm	Leonard Gaunt
THE 35 mm SINGLE LENS REFLEX	Leonard Gaunt
	Processing
CIBACHROME	Jack H. Coote
COLOUR FILM PROCESSING	Derek Watkins
COLOUR PRINTING	Jack H. Coote
ENLARGING	Günter Spitzing
HOME PROCESSING	Ralph Jacobson
THE DARKROOM	Leonard Gaunt
	Subjects
ACTION PHOTOGRAPHY	Don Morley
MOUNTAINS	Douglas Milner
PHOTOGRAPHING PEOPLE	Alison Trapmore
PORTRAITS	Günter Spitzing
CLOSE-UPS	Sidney Ray
	Movie
MOVIEMAKING	Paul Petzold
SHOOTING ANIMATION	Zoran Perisic

The FOCALGUIDE to the Darkroom

Leonard Gaunt

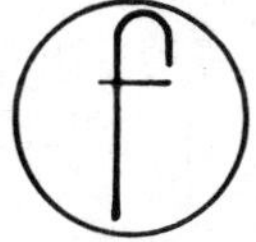

Focal Press · London

Focal/Hastings House · New York

BL British Library Cataloguing in Publication Data

Gaunt, Leonard
The focalguide to the darkroom.
1. Photography–Processing
I. Title
770'.28 TR287

ISBN (except USA) 0 240 51005 4
ISBN (USA only) 0 8038 2365 7

Text phototypeset by Computer Photoset Ltd., Birmingham

Printed in Great Britain
by Thomson Litho Ltd, East Kilbride, Scotland

Contents

Introduction

Once you start taking photography seriously, a darkroom becomes a necessity. You are no longer satisfied with the small prints provided by D & P services. You want larger prints; you want to print from only part of the negative or slide; you want better prints—the kind of print that only individual attention can provide. Happily, you can now make them in colour as well as black and white; but most home processing and printing is still in black and white. The basic set-up is much the same in either case but there are a few differences. In this book we discuss both methods.

The difficulty for most people, in this era of the small house or flat, is in finding space in which to locate the darkroom. Many ingenious suggestions have been put forward in photographic magazines and elsewhere for making use of even the smallest spaces—from cupboards to alcoves to attics and even a corner of bedroom or living room. Naturally, if you have a spare room or a large garden shed or a garage or half of a garage that is available for this purpose you are in luck. You can then build a permanent workroom rather than the temporary set-up so often needed in other locations.

Wherever you put your darkroom, you run across the same problems—although they may be more acute in some circumstances. You have to deal with electrical wiring, plumbing, waste disposal and space saving. You have to think hard about the type of equipment to obtain. Is an exposure timer really necessary? What about an exposure meter? What size dishes should you buy? In what quantities do you buy paper and chemicals? Should you buy film in bulk? How do you store materials? Do you need temperature and voltage control? Is a running water supply necessary? How do you weatherproof and heat an outside darkroom? How do you make temporary blackouts for windows?

This book attempts to answer all these questions and many more.

It tends to generalize because it is impossible to give specific recommendations for all kinds of windows, all shapes of room, all varieties of garage and shed, and so on. Nevertheless, it gives honest advice on the many problems you will meet, based on the practical experience of the author and on the solutions that other people have found to similar problems.

Think it out first!

Setting up a permanent darkroom is not a task to be undertaken lightly or in a hurry. It is advisable to think carefully about the layout, blackout methods, heating, ventilation, electricity and water supply, and other such matters. They involve a lot of work and have a considerable effect on the comfort and, indeed, safety of your working conditions. Nor, in a state of euphoria at finding yourself with room for a permanent set-up, should you decide that every darkroom gadget available thereby becomes a necessity. The more you spend on 'aids to better printing' the less you have available for paper and chemicals—the essentials that provide the practical experience that is the best aid of all.

Most people, at least in the beginning, have to carry out their darkroom activities in a confined space—more often than not the bathroom—that is available only at certain times and in which they have to set up their equipment before starting and clear it away again when they are finished. We shall deal with the problems of this type of darkroom first.

Temporary Locations

The most popular location for the temporary darkroom appears to be the bathroom – probably because it has running water and there really does not seem to be anywhere else that is suitable. The choice is, in fact, rather a strange one. It must be almost impossible for anybody with a family, for example, to monopolize the bathroom for a lengthy period without causing other members of the family inconvenience and possibly arousing resentment – especially when the bathroom also houses the lavatory. If it were not for the fact that the bathroom has running water, it would logically seem to be about the last place in which to carry on spare-time activities.

Yet running water comes very low indeed in the list of necessities for a darkroom – at least for part-timers working in their own homes. So let us consider the problem of water supplies first, as it seems to have such an undue influence on the thinking of so many people about to set up their own darkroom facilities.

Water supplies

Water is, of course, a necessity for photographic processing and, in the final stages, running water is, though not necessary, certainly very convenient. Prints and films can be washed satisfactorily – and perhaps even more efficiently – in several changes of water, but it is a tedious business. Until you reach the final wash stage, however, whether in film processing or in printing, you have absolutely no need for running water at all.

Undoubtedly, it is useful to have a supply of water in the darkroom but it does not have to be on tap. There are innumerable types of liquid container that can be pressed into service, from the one or two litre plastic bottles that soft drinks, washing up liquids, etc. are supplied in, to 12 litre and larger barrels or cubitainers for wine storage and similar uses. Many of the larger containers are fitted with effective taps and filler holes—or the tap may be removable for fillin', purposes.

An inexpensive type of container has been available for many years from camping stores. It is a strong polythene bag with stretcher rods and a cutout at one end to form a carrying handle. It holds about six litres and is fitted with an efficient tap of the push-fit type. It can be carried easily from the water supply to the darkroom, where the stretcher rods allow it to be hung on stout hooks.

Probably the best type of container for a temporary darkroom that has to be constantly set up and dismantled is, however, a simple wide-mouthed jug or bottle (or more than one) that can be carried without effort and easily poured from without splashing. It is not a good idea to make up solutions in the processing dishes and then carry them to and from the darkroom area. That positively invites spillage. If you return the solutions to storage bottles in the darkroom, use a funnel. Pour any solutions you discard while you are working into a bucket.

Thus, the absence of running water need not affect your decision as to the suitability of any particular location for darkroom work. Finished prints can be stored in a bucket or bowl of water for washing at the end of the printing session.

Working in the bathroom

Having made it clear that the bathroom is not a very sensible choice as a location for a darkroom—and we shall have more to say about that yet—we must, nevertheless, cater for those perverse people who prefer not to take our advice. Naturally, bathrooms vary considerably in size and shape but, these days, they tend to be small. Floor space is often limited and rarely provides enough room to set up a bench or table to hold the enlarger and processing dishes. The most popular method of operation for those who use large dishes (20 × 26 cm upward) is to locate them on a wooden tray-like structure placed on top of the bath. Sometimes the enlarger has to go alongside them on the same structure but that is not at all a good idea. Apart from space saving, the reasoning behind this location seems to be that splashes will run harmlessly down the drain. Nothing could be farther from the truth! In most bathrooms, it would be far preferable to let the splashes hit the floor, which is likely to be of a type that can be easily mopped up. Trickles of developer and fixer running down the bath, on the other hand, can leave very nasty stains that can turn out to be practically irremovable, while some of the solutions used in colour printing can make an awful mess of metal fitments.

It is not a good idea to locate the enlarger over the bath for two reasons. First, it is difficult to make sure it is very rigidly supported, so it might finish up in the bottom of the bath. If that has water in it —as it should have—the resulting fireworks could be spectacular. Secondly, few baths give a comfortable working height for the enlarger baseboard and the result of a prolonged printing session is likely to be severe back pain. You might, of course, sit down to operate the enlarger but you cannot sit all the time and, with space at a premium, there is a fair chance that, at some later stage, you will fall over the chair or stool that you have pushed aside so that you can more easily reach the processing dishes. The sitting posture may not be all that comfortable, either, because baths are not normally constructed with kneeholes.

In finding an alternative location, however, make sure that the support for the enlarger is completely rigid. Apart from any risk of shake or vibration while making the print, there is, again, the possibility that you might knock it over and break or damage electrical connections. Do not balance it on a chair or flimsy table.

It is a relatively simple matter to make up a support from four timber pieces of about 25–35 mm square section cut to the required baseboard height and fastened all round, top and bottom, with timber battens so that the baseboard can rest securely on top. You can even cover the sides and back with hardboard, put a door on the front and shelves inside to form a complete storage unit that might take the enlarger too if it is small and dismantlable.

The height of the baseboard is a matter of personal preference but most people find that ordinary table or desk height is too low. A height of about a metre or 3 feet is generally suitable for people of average height. Be careful, however, if the ceiling is low. Some enlargers need a lot of headroom and you may have to locate the baseboard rather lower than you would like so that the enlarger head can reach the top of its column.

Your set-up in the bathroom, therefore, should consist of the enlarger on a rigid base away from the bath and your processing dishes on a flat level surface firmly braced on the top of the bath—assuming that there is not room to put them anywhere else. Run a little water into the bath so that any spilt liquids that do escape will not sit in the bottom of the bath doing their best to destroy the enamel. This water can also serve as a depository for the finished prints until you are ready to wash them at the end of the printing session.

Blacking out

Excluding light from your working area is a problem in any kind of makeshift darkroom. No general rules can be laid down because windows vary in size, shape and availability of flat surfaces to which to fasten blackout material. The two most suitable materials are heavy duty black plastic sheeting and hardboard—that most versatile, thin but tough composition board that is so valuable to any handyman.

The greatest problem is in making a light-tight seal at the edges. Hardboard on a timber frame tailored to the size of the window opening provides a perfect blackout if you can devise a simple, inconspicuous method of attaching it to the window frame. Sometimes, this type of frame can be held quite securely with two or three small timber wedges at the bottom. If you have a generously sized window ledge, one or two timber supports hinged on the centre line of the frame may be similarly wedged at the bottom. If there is woodwork available at the sides, you might drill small holes into which dowel-type pegs can be pushed. The disadvantage of any hardboard frame, however, is that it is bulky and difficult to store inconspicuously.

Plastic sheeting can be used in a similar manner but, as it has the advantage that it can be rolled up when not in use, it is better to fasten it to top and bottom battens only. The side battens can then be force-fitted into position on assembly. With care, the force-fitting can also hold the frame in place. Alternatively, you can attach the sheeting directly to the window frame by means of press-studs

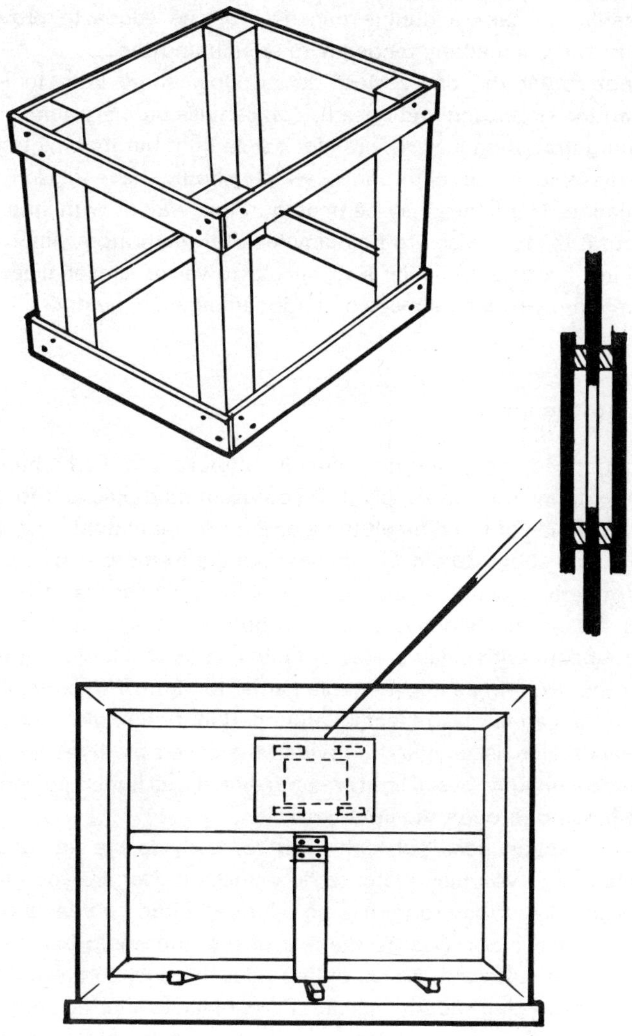

You need only a saw, hammer and nails to make a sturdy enlarger support. The hardboard blackout *(bottom)* is fitted into a recessed window and supported by wedges at the bottom. Extra support is provided by a central strut if necessary. Details of the ventilator are given in the text.

or strips of the Velcro type of tear-off fastening material. It is advisable to make a double thickness at the edges to provide rigidity and combat any tendency to stretch and sag.

Do not forget the door. Most doors allow some light to leak around the edges and underneath. You can use ordinary commercial draughtproofing materials to block such light but that might not be advisable in all bathrooms, which should have reasonable ventilation. The edges may be treated in this way or with strips of felt but it is often easier to treat any leaks at the bottom simply by blocking it off temporarily with an old towel or similar piece of material or by leaning a piece of hardboard against the door.

Letting the air in

Light-trapped ventilation may already be present in the bathroom. If not, you must try to supply it. If you use a rigid blackout for the window, it is not too difficult to incorporate a ventilator into it. Cut a hole, say about 30 cm (12 inches) square in the board in front of an opening window and cover it with larger pieces of board, about 50 cm or 18 inches square on both sides, spaced from the central board with small pieces of timber so as to allow a passage for air but to form an impenetrable barrier for light. The principle is that light cannot be reflected around two rightangles (not by ordinary materials, anyway). Provided the covers are large enough to prevent oblique rays of light entering directly, all light is prevented from passing through the light trap.

Plastic sheeting does not lend itself so easily to the fitting of a ventilator and you may prefer to do without it. Nor are you much better off if your bathroom has no window. Fitting a ventilator to the door may not appeal to the rest of the household but it may well be that sufficient air can enter under the door to prevent the air from becoming too foul inside. If you really cannot fit adequate ventilation, do not spend too long in the darkroom at a stretch. There is no real danger with the normal chemicals but the fumes and the stale air can give you quite a thick head—especially if you smoke. Open the door occasionally, say every 40 minutes or so, and take a break.

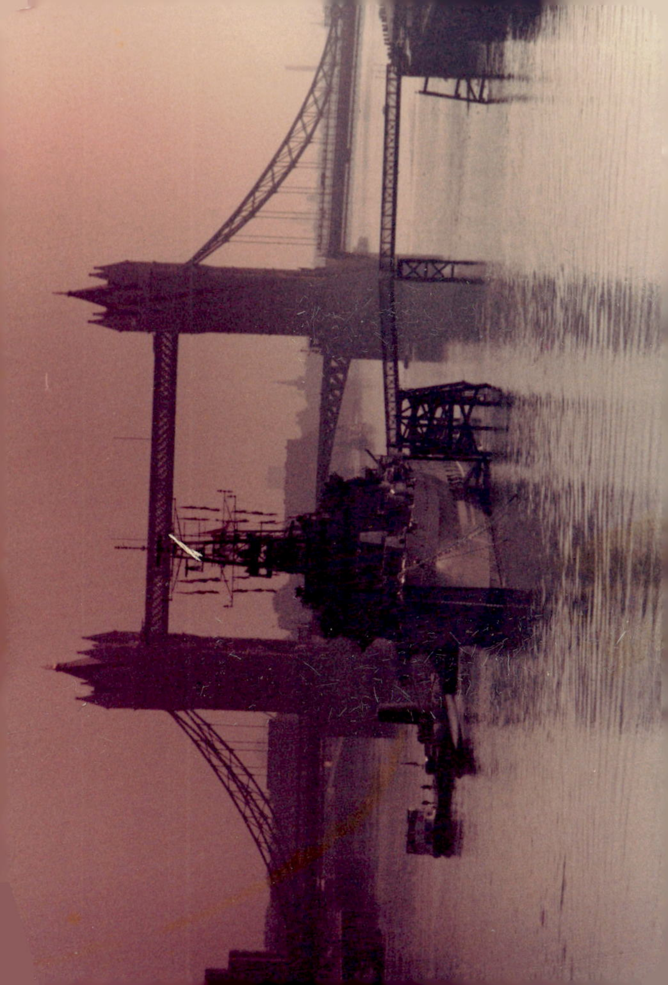

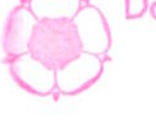

Date of Photo: Christmas 1978

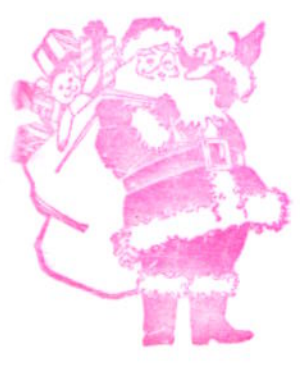

Post-a-Photo PERSONALIZED POSTCARD & GREETING CARD
U.K. Patent No. 1424634 by Tudor Processing Limited.

PLACE
STAMP
HERE

Post Card

Electricity and earthing

One thing you have to have in your darkroom is electricity–and that is one of the biggest arguments against using the bathroom. Bathrooms tend to hold dampness and may have metal fittings that are very efficiently earthed via the water pipes. When you use electrical equipment in the presence of other items that are well earthed, it is advisable, if not imperative, that all your equipment is also earthed. If, by mischance or carelessness, any exposed metal part of your equipment should become 'live' and you should be in contact both with the faulty equipment and with an earthed item, a powerful electric current will find its way to earth through your body. Its passage is accelerated if your hands are damp, if the floor is solid (and even more so if it is also damp) and if your equipment is not fused or has fuses of too high a rating. That could be lethal. Bathrooms are not, or should not be, fitted with earthed electrical sockets and it is likely, therefore, that you will connect your enlarger to the light socket, which may or may not provide an earth. A safer arrangement is to connect the enlarger to the only type of socket that should be allowed in a bathroom–the shaver socket. If of an approved design, that contains an isolating transformer and fuse that should prevent any heavy current passing. The shaver socket will take your enlarger lamp satisfactorily (it is generally rated at about one amp) but do not plug anything else into it.

Under no circumstances should you fit any other type of electrical outlet into your bathroom, nor should you run in a temporary supply from an outside socket. Any switches you fit to enlarger, safelight, etc. should be of the remote, cord-pull type. Preferably, do not use the bathroom at all.

Protecting the floor

The majority of photographers do not have exclusive use of a bathroom or do not want to use it as a darkroom for the reasons already discussed. So, they have to find another location for a temporary darkroom. One of the biggest problems in that case is the protection of walls, floors, carpets, furniture, etc. from the ravages of splashes from the water supply and worse. If you can manage to block off the corner of a living room, bedroom or hall, you are unfortunate if it is carpeted, because that calls for immediate protective measures. A carpet attacked by frequent splashing with developer and fixer, not to mention bleach, is not a pretty sight.

The simplest form of protection is a large plastic tray—the largest you can obtain or accommodate—from your nearest supplier of garden equipment or pets' products. They are supplied as gravel trays or seed trays and are not very expensive. It need not be a deep tray—just enough to allow a little paddling about in your processing dishes or careless placing of the print tongs without contaminating the working surface or allowing liquids to ooze along to the edges and thence to the floor. If you work on a table against the wall, it might be as well to protect the wall-covering, too, by leaning the ubiquitous piece of hardboard or other surfaced board against it. If you feel at all doubtful about the floor area, cover it entirely with a large sheet of hardboard.

Providing additional blackout

If you use part of a living room or bedroom for your darkroom, temporary blacking-out is difficult and sometimes impossible, or at best impracticable, in daylight. If the room has heavy curtains or not too large windows, however, it is just about possible to put extra curtaining in your chosen corner by suspending it from the ceiling on runners. There are various types of flexible runner that can be curved quite sharply and allow the curtains to run smoothly if you keep the rail lubricated with a silicone polish. Fastening to the ceiling can be tricky. You must screw the supporting brackets into the beams, not into plasterboard or the laths of a plaster ceiling. The curtain or curtains must be backed with light-excluding material and must brush the ceiling and drag on the floor. You are left, of course, with the curtain rail on the ceiling and the curtains on the wall when you clear away—but you cannot have everything. It is possible for such curtaining to exclude daylight if you use really heavy duty material and put a deep pelmet over the curtain rail. In most cases it should be possible to exclude low-level artificial light if you have to use the room when it is occupied. The only alternative is to black out the whole room and that is not generally practicable unless you have a room for your exclusive use.

Seeking alternative locations

When neither bathroom nor a corner of another room is available, you have to examine the house for nooks and crannies. The tiny areas in which many keen photographers have been able to cram their darkrooms are almost unbelievable. Among the smallest I have heard of are a caravan shower cubicle with a floor area of about 56 × 140 cm and a loo measuring about 1.6 × 1 m.

The older house may well have a cupboard that large or a reasonable amount of spare floor space at the head of the stairs. There is almost certain to be some room under the stairs. A flat may well have an entrance hall with no windows. The main thing to look for is an area that can be easily blacked out. The disadvantage you generally have to accept is that it may be impossible to provide adequate ventilation.

Blacking out part of an area can be dealt with by the suspended curtaining already described but you have to look for a source of electricity. Do not rely on plugging your equipment into a single socket—especially a light socket—via multiple adaptors. That leads to a dangerous profusion of trailing cables. Use a multiple socket extension as described in the section on electrical wiring. Then you can have several sockets available in your makeshift darkroom and only one lead coming in from outside.

Using the available space

In all temporary locations, space-saving is vital—even if your working area is relatively large. You need your equipment to occupy as little space as possible so that it can be rapidly set up and just as rapidly cleared away. You may be perfectly happy to spend a little time getting your equipment ready at the beginning of a printing session but it is quite possible that you will go on printing longer than you intended. You are then rather tired and, if the session did not go too well (it happens to all of us) clearing away becomes an irritating chore. The more compact your set-up and the more methodical your approach, the quicker you can clear up. One of the most useful items for a temporary darkroom is a tea-trolley or similar arrangement of trays on wheels. Tack hardboard to three sides of the trays to enclose the area between them. You do not need to be too much of a handyman to put an extra tray or shelf in if there is enough room. Then you have a storage area that might enable you to pack the whole darkroom into a mobile cupboard that just has to be wheeled into position when you need it. If you can put doors on it, so much the better. You are commonly advised not to store paper and chemicals together in such an arrangement but in this modern age we have such materials as cling film and baking foil that can offer perfect protection to your sensitized materials.

You might even get your enlarger into such an arrangement because there is at least one enlarger on the market that packs away into a surprisingly small case and others are designed to take apart for storage in their original packing. In the working area, the top tray can accommodate three reasonably-sized processing dishes but it might be a good idea to resurface it if necessary with a plastic laminate and possibly to heighten the edge both to contain any solution spillage and to ensure that the dishes are not pushed over the edge.

Shelving arrangements

Your basic requirements in the darkroom are space for the enlarger, processing dishes, paper, water, developer and fixer storage bottles, measuring flasks, safelights and a bucket or bowl of water in which to deposit the finished prints. You may have more equipment than that, but those are the essentials. Almost inevitably, you need at least one shelf, whether of the type fixed to the wall (permanently or on tracks) or a temporary board supported on whatever happens to be available. That takes the intermittently or seldom used items like paper, bottles of solution and measures. It might even take the safelight and clock or other timing device. Then you need a support for the enlarger and somewhere to put your

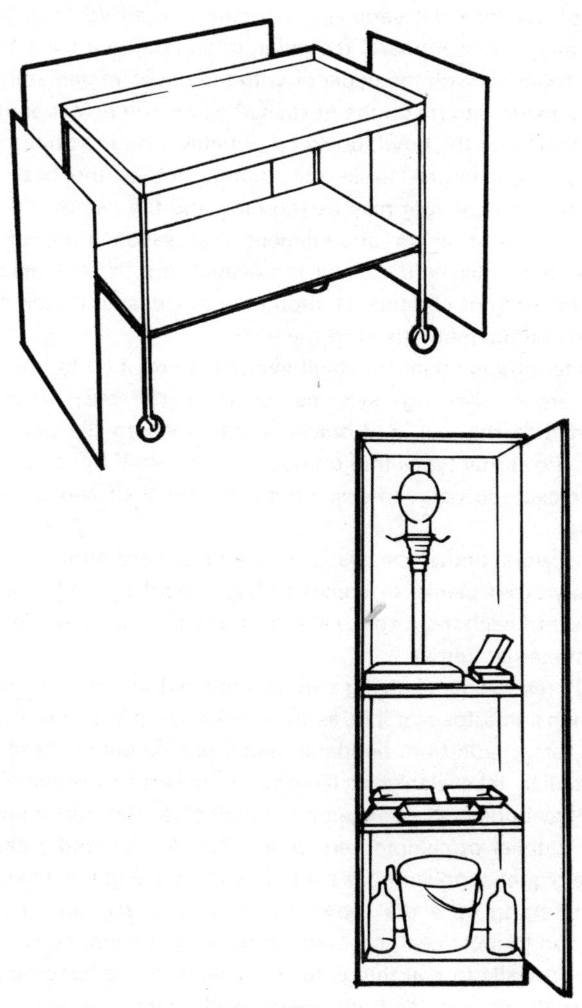

A tea trolley makes a useful mobile darkroom bench. With the sides enclosed, it can even provide storage space for all your equipment.
Do not overlook the vertical arrangement *(bottom)* when space is limited.

processing dishes. Both of these items need to be reasonably solid and stable and may take one of the forms already described.

Do not overlook the vertical arrangement. If all you can find is a deep alcove or cupboard, the enlarger can be on a solid top shelf either together with the paper or with the paper immediately below it. The dishes can go on the next shelf down (on no account above the paper) and the bowl, bucket or whatever on the floor, together with storage bottles, flasks etc. It may not be the best way of working—the enlarger may be too high and the dishes too low for comfort—but it is an arrangement that saves a lot of space. Shelving of this type can be removable, too, if it is made from blockboard (not chipboard) supported at sides and back on solid battens permanently fixed to the wall.

A neater arrangement for small shelves is provided by the various commercial shelving systems using perforated metal strips attached to the wall and brackets that slot into the perforations. There are sturdy types that do not need the shelf to be attached to the bracket; so you can easily remove both shelf and brackets for storage.

If you work under the stairs, shelving is very simple. You nail suitably sized planks or pieces of blockboard to the underside of the riser of each tread (or to alternate treads if you want to accommodate larger items).

Totally removable shelving can be provided in many ways. There are such items, for example, as shoe racks, camp kitchens, vegetable racks, etc. made from bendable metal rod. Many of these can be adapted to take planks or lengths of shelving to provide a free-standing bookshelf arrangement suitable for the odd items. Your local supplier of camping equipment (or the mail order catalogue of the bigger suppliers) has a lot of items you might like to consider when setting up a darkroom. You have a space-saving problem common to most campers—and particularly the tenting types, who have no walls to nail things to. They tend to use hanging storage units with pockets and you might well adapt their ideas to your darkroom. Why not store paper boxes or packets, bottles, etc. in hanging pockets?

A little ingenuity goes a long way in setting up a darkroom. Do not be hidebound by common photographic practice as propounded in the magazines or even in this book. Improvize as much as possible and look for items to suit your location instead of trying to adapt available photographic items to that purpose. Apart from the gardening centre and the camping goods supplier, there are many do-it-yourself stores and hardware shops that stock items you might find useful. Even the home-brewing specialists have siphons, taps, racks, measures, containers and so on that can be adapted to photographic use and might just solve your particular problem. We shall have more to say about such matters because many problems are common to both the temporary and the permanent darkroom.

Permanent Locations

You are fortunate indeed if you have room to set up a permanent darkroom and you must not waste your good fortune by dashing in with chair and table and an improvised blackout. Whether your available location be spare room, attic, garage, shed or whatever, it is unlikely to be so perfectly adapted to photographic use as to need no modification. It is not likely to be easily lightproofed and well ventilated. The electrical outputs, if any, are almost certainly unsuitably located. The floor covering may well need modification, and so on.

Blackout and ventilation

The first thing to consider is the blacking out of windows and doors. If you are choosing between one location and another (such as which end of the garage) you will normally choose the one without windows or with the smaller windows—but not always. It is, after all, much easier to put a ventilator in a window than in a wall. If there is no simple way to ventilate the room, you may well prefer to keep the window. Then again, a larger window in one room might be an easier one to black out than an odd-shaped smaller one.

We have dealt with blackout methods to some extent in the previous chapter and the methods suggested there are quite suitable for the more permanent location. On the other hand if the darkroom is to be used for that purpose only, you can make more permanent arrangements. This does not necessarily mean that you will black the window out permanently. You could remove the glass and replace it with opaque material but that is rather more drastic treatment than most people would wish to tolerate in a room that may one day need to be converted back to normal use.

You can, depending on the money available, fit a commercially-produced roller blind tailored to the window size. Those made specifically for darkroom use are expensive but efficient and convenient. Other types and do-it-yourself versions may not be fully light proof unless, in the latter case, you are a better-than-average handyman. Similarly, in a permanent set-up, you may be able to justify the expense of a commercially-produced ventilator. Various versions are available for darkroom use.

The larger the room, the less you have to worry about ventilation and—to some extent—blackout. If, for example, you have a room $2\frac{1}{2}$ m (8 feet) or so long and of such construction that the door can be at one end while your light-sensitive materials are always handled at the other end, it will not matter too much if the door is ill-fitting. Small gaps should not admit enough light to worry about, especially if furniture, dark surfaces, etc. can be arranged to absorb most of the light that is admitted.

The extent of your blackout is largely a matter of common sense. If, in the area where you use light-sensitive materials, you can see nothing at all after ten minutes with all the lights out, the area should be safe. It does not matter if, when you turn round, you can see glimmers of light at the other end of the room. If your darkroom activity is confined to making black-and-white prints, your blackout is not particularly critical. For colour printing, or handling films, though, it must be considerably better.

Safelighting

The darkroom should not be dark. You can handle all normal black-and-white printing papers in bright light of the correct colour. Note that we say papers—not films. Despite the fact that black-and-white films cannot produce coloured images, they are, with few exceptions, sensitive to light of all colours. They are panchromatic. The original photographic films were sensitive only to blue light and were unable to produce faithful tonal renderings of all colours. Red was rendered too dark, for example, because it had virtually no effect on the film.

Photographic paper, on the other hand, is generally sensitive to light only in the blue-green area of the spectrum—and not too much green at that. It is quite blind to light at the red end and to most mixtures of red and green and can therefore safely be exposed to reasonably bright yellowy-brown light. Darkroom lighting takes advantage of this colour blindness.

A safelight is a simple light-box holding a 15, 25 or 40-watt bulb according to size. One side has an opening into which you can place the required safelight filter, available in standard sizes of 5 × 7 inches and 8 × 10 inches. The filter itself is often a sandwich construction of coloured gelatin or acetate, opal glass for diffusion and plain glass. You can light your darkroom almost brilliantly through such a filter with perfect safety but it is advisable, nevertheless to keep the safelight about a metre or so (3-4 feet) from your enlarger and processing dishes. Take careful note of the maximum lamp wattage allowed. If you exceed it, you could produce cracks in the gelatin and destroy its safelight characteristics.

It is not necessary and is, in fact, undesirable to darken the walls and ceiling of a darkroom. They should preferably be white or of a pastel shade because, no matter what colour they are, they cannot reflect light of any colour not contained in the safelighting. If they are strongly coloured or black, however, they can absorb a considerable amount of light and reduce the overall illumination. Ideally, you should be able to move around your darkroom with ease and should not have to fumble with any part of your equipment because of lack of light.

Layout of working areas

It is worth giving a great deal of thought to the layout of a permanent darkroom—especially if space is limited or you intend to crowd in a lot of equipment. Second thoughts can involve virtually tearing the whole room to pieces again. We dealt with space-saving in the previous chapter, so the following comments are aimed more specifically at those not suffering unduly from such limitations.

First, think about the type of work you intend to do. There are two obvious bench space requirements—for the enlarger and for the processing dishes. These are often referred to as the dry bench and the wet bench and never the twain are supposed to meet; but that does imply a degree of gay abandon to which the amateur is not usually prone. Splashing solutions all over his own property is not likely to appeal to him so much as to, perhaps, a somewhat disgruntled laboratory worker. It can be very inconvenient to cross the room between enlarger and processing dishes for every print, whereas in the lab, of course, somebody else might want to use the enlarger. If you have sufficient space, there is no reason why the enlarger and the dishes should not be on the same bench provided they do not actually jostle shoulders.

Another important space requirement is for cutting paper. Buying paper in small sizes is uneconomic. It is much better to cut larger sizes down as required. You can carry out the cutting on the enlarger baseboard but it is much more convenient to set aside a separate area if you have the room.

Storage space is vital and, as time goes on, you will find that you need much more than you originally considered necessary. If your darkroom is small, you may have a problem but most permanent locations can provide enough room for shelves above and below the workbenches. The floor below the workbench is the most convenient place to store large containers of solutions. At least one reasonably light-tight cupboard is advisable for the storage of papers, films, filters, lenses and other relatively fragile items.

Shelving and cupboards are relatively easy for the experienced handyman to construct, but they can be a nightmare for others. If you are one of those whose shelves invariably fall off the wall under the weight of a paper clip, the hints on hammer and nail woodwork in the next chapter may help you. Alternatively, you may be able to find free-standing units that will serve the same purpose. Discarded small bookshelf units or bedside lockers may even be stood on top of the worksurface if you have sufficient room.

Keep the area by the door as clear as possible, especially if the door opens inward. You may want to get bulky equipment or furniture in at some future date and shelving within a foot or so of the door edge can be an annoying obstacle. If your room is rather small, it is worth investigating the possibility of changing the door to outward-opening or of fitting a sliding door—preferably on the outside.

Your paper and negative storage cupboard, filing cabinet, boxes or whatever, should be located as near to the enlarger as possible. Most people seem to keep the paper in its original packets and extract sheets as required. There are paper safes on the market and it is possible to construct a light-tight drawer under the bench or the enlarger baseboard, but these arrangements are really more suitable for those who use a lot of paper. It is difficult to feel too confident about paper sitting in a drawer or paper safe for several weeks.

If you cut larger paper, you may prefer to cut a few sheets as you go along and store the smaller pieces in a separate box kept for the purpose. The cabinets used for card file indexes are useful in this respect. With the paper inside a reasonably light tight box and the box in a card file drawer, there is little risk of light intruding and the paper is immediately to hand.

If there is any tendency to dampness in your darkroom you must protect paper and negatives—a subject we deal with more fully when considering outside locations. Similarly, do not leave open dishes of solutions lying about. The solutions evaporate and distribute chemical vapour and possibly dust about the room. That cannot be of any benefit to light-sensitive materials or to lenses. If you do leave solutions in dishes for any length of time, fit the dishes with heavy lids made from surfaced blockboard, marine plywood or similar material.

Having decided on the amount of working surface you require—and it may also include space for a dryer/glazer, room to hang films to dry, a small area where you make notes, calculations, etc.—plan the various positions for the equipment carefully. Take some note of the position of the electrical power points, if any, but do not let them influence the layout unduly. You will almost certainly need additional sockets and you will find instructions in the next chapter for providing them. We are assuming that you do not intend to introduce running water and drainage. If you do, you will find some plumbing hints in the next chapter, too.

Siting the enlarger

The enlarger position is important. Unless you have health problems, it is advisable to operate the enlarger standing up. A sitting position can demand too much room and reduces your mobility. The height of the baseboard should then be in the region of about 80 cm or 32 inches, rather higher than the average table or desk. That is a convenient height for the processing dishes, too. The baseboard height may be governed, however, by the length of the column and the height of the ceiling—again a problem more often met with in outside locations.

If your enlarger has a limited column height bear in mind the possibility that you may want to make enlargements beyond its normal capability. That can be achieved by swinging the enlarger head round the column to project over the back of the baseboard, or by turning the head sideways to project on to a vertical surface. Position your enlarger so that this is possible. If you intend to project on to a wall, place the enlarger at a suitable distance from it and do not put shelves, safelight, etc. on that wall. A suitable arrangement might, in fact, place the processing dishes between the enlarger and the wall.

The enlarger baseboard can sometimes be a cumbersome obstacle to comfortable working. It projects from the smooth working surface. Investigate the possibilities of doing away with it. It is often possible to mount the column directly on the work surface. This should preferably be effected by bolting the column right through the work surface and through a stout metal plate underneath. Or it might be possible to mount the column on the wall. If you do that, you can even increase its height slightly above the baseboard. In all such cases, however, make sure that the column is truly perpendicular to the work surface or, in the case of sloping columns, that the negative carrier is completely parallel with the work surface.

Outside locations

If your darkroom is in an outside garage or shed or even in the roof space, you may have additional problems caused by low or sloping ceilings, penetration of cold and damp and difficulty in providing adequate blackout. You may also have to do a lot more construction work in the way of cladding walls, erecting partitions, installing electricity and so on. On the other hand, you may have more freedom in using the space. Except in the case of roof spaces, which can have very awkward shapes, your working area is likely to be regular in shape with no protruding chimney breasts, window ledges, etc. It might have plenty of available timber to fasten things to with a simple hammer and nail technique.

If you do use an outside location, assume from the outset that it will be damp and cold—in temperate or worse climates at any rate. In summer it may well become unbearably hot but you have to think more about your materials and equipment than personal comfort. So, when you plan to clad walls and ceiling, remember that you need insulation, particularly against damp, which can affect light-sensitive materials severely and can effectively destroy negatives and slides. In fact, unless you can provide perfect insulation, which is unlikely, it is inadvisable to store negatives and slides in darkrooms. Keep them in filing boxes or other containers in a warm dry place indoors and take them into the darkroom only when you intend to use them.

Apart from insulation, which we deal with in the next chapter, there are various precautions against damp that you can take inside the darkroom. Plastic bags and cling film are useful for wrapping most items. Enlarger lenses are often supplied in plastic cases that are adequate protection for most purposes. When leaving the darkroom always detach the lens from the enlarger and store it in its case.

Impregnated paper of the type used for wrapping tools can be bought in sheets and attached to walls, shelves, etc. close to metal objects or structures such as the enlarger. It offers good protection up to about 30 cm (12 inches) or so from its surface. Silica gel is a useful drying agent to place in cupboards, cabinets, etc. where you keep film or paper.

A particularly useful item in an outside darkroom is an old refrigerator. If you have to replace your fridge do not scrap the old one. Put it in the darkroom. It makes a fine, more or less airtight cupboard for the storage of paper, negatives and even bottles of solution if they are thoroughly sealed against the emission of fumes. If you are in any doubt about that, wrap your paper packets or boxes in cling film.

You might consider putting a serviceable refrigerator in the darkroom for storing colour materials but for the hobby or occasional worker that can be more of a nuisance than an asset. You suddenly decide to use the darkroom and then remember that your materials are in the fridge and need airing for an hour or two to reach room temperature. If you do not do that, warm air could condense on the cold paper surface and cause all sorts of trouble.

The same thing applies to glass. If you have a cold darkroom, inside or out, watch out for condensation on the enlarger lens when you turn on the heating.

An outside location may be erected on a concrete base, forming a very cold and probably damp floor. There are various ways of treating that. The simplest is to cover the floor with sheets of hardboard. Depending on the dampness of the floor, you can lay the hardboard untreated or paint the underside with a bitumen-based paint or other damproofing solution. A good treatment for the concrete itself, particularly against dusting, is waterglass—the stuff that was once used for preserving eggs. It will seal almost any porous surface.

If you are more ambitious or the floor is very damp, you could duckboard it or even wooden floor it completely, ie, place beams (5 × 7 cm minimum) across the floor at about 30 cm separation and nail 5 or 7 cm slats with small gaps between them or unspaced floorboards across the beams. The beams at least should be of rotproof timber or should be suitably treated before laying. Alternatively, you can try the type of flooring used in caravans and boats, with an insulating undersurface of polystyrene.

Carpeting on the floor can also reduce heat loss and keep the feet warmer but it is better not to carpet the areas that might receive water or solution spillage.

Arrangement of the various working surfaces may be easier in an outside location but it does raise a few problems of its own. Garages and sheds can have sloping roofs. There is no very great problem if the roof is flat with a slight slope for drainage. Just bear in mind that one end is higher than the other. When the roof is V-shaped, however the side walls are often rather low. Depending on your own height and the height of the enlarger column, that may make it necessary, or at least more comfortable, to place your working surface across the V and locate your enlarger in the middle of it. If your door happens to be in the V-wall, as it usually is, you are left with just one obligatory wall for your workbench.

If you have a choice of three walls, place your enlarger as far away as possible from door and windows in case you have any trouble with light-trapping. If there is any difference, choose the wall most suitable for attaching a solid bench and possibly shelves. It is generally preferable to run the bench right along one wall. Again, do not be unduly influenced by the position of electricity supply sockets, if any. The next chapter deals with their location and extension.

Planning the ideal

Ideals are individual and my ideal darkroom may not be yours. They also depend on the kind of work to be carried out in the darkroom and the availability of equipment. Nevertheless, we can try to envisage what we would like to have and perhaps adapt a few of the ideal arrangements to suit our less-than-ideal surroundings.

We shall deal here with the internal layout rather than the construction because it goes without saying that the ideal darkroom has perfect light-trapping, insulation and ventilation. Inside, it measures 250 cm (about 8 feet) square or larger. It has a door, either opening outward or sliding, almost in one corner. The wall opposite the door (call it the end wall) and the one not adjacent to the door (the left hand wall) have benches running their full length with a height of about 80 cm and a depth of about 75 cm. The enlarger is located toward one end of the left-hand bench but with space to allow projection to the end wall. The space allows you to make notes or house negatives or paper temporarily. It may also accommodate the enlarger transformer, meter, etc.

On the other side of the enlarger is a small cabinet with drawers or trays to accommodate your negative and slide store (or part of it) and sufficient paper for your immediate requirements.

A little further down the bench are three processing dishes for black and white work, followed by a small sink let into the work surface with hot and cold water, or cold water and a wall heater. The sink is drained to an outside soakaway or gulley connected to the house drains.

On the wall behind this bench is a shelf running from the sink end

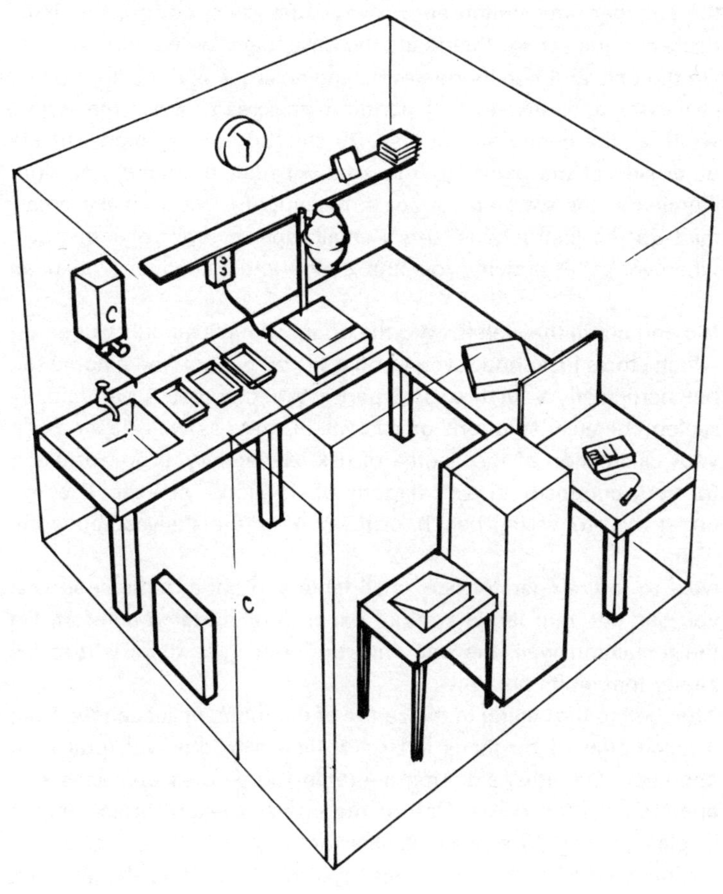

The ‘ideal’ darkroom described in the text. Safelighting should be on the ceiling or on a wall not too close to the enlarger or processing dishes.

to the enlarger. It accommodates measuring flasks, thermometers, small bottles of solution, print tongs, lens cases, enlarger negative carriers and the various other odds and ends that a darkroom soon accumulates. Above it, near the processing dishes, is an electric clock with a sweep second hand. Below it, behind the enlarger, is the enlarger time switch and/or exposure meter control box connected to the sensor that reads the baseboard illumination.

On the end wall bench, nearest to the enlarger, is the colour paper processor and next to it a partition or screen across the whole width of the bench and at least 75 cm (30 inches) high. On the other side of the partition, a low-power fully shrouded strip light illuminates the working surface sufficiently for you to make notes, read up the instructions, use a small tape recorder or indulge in whatever other activity you find useful and for which you need light.

Moving down the wall toward the door, we have an old refrigerator which stores just about everything else you cannot find a home for, but particularly your boxes of paper. Whether you store suitably sealed chemical solutions or packets in there as well depends on your calculation of the degree of risk. Certainly you do not use it for your current bottles or flagons of developer or fixer. They go under the processing bench, or if small, on the shelves above the dishes.

Next to the refrigerator is a small table and paper trimmer so that you can cut your larger sizes of paper in uncluttered comfort. On the remaining wall, the one with the door in it, there is a space heater that emits no light.

Attached to the ceiling in the centre of the room, or suspended from it, according to height is a 10 × 8 inch safelight with pull cord operation. On either side of it are three-foot fluorescent tubes also operated by pull cords. One of the cords is taken through metal or plastic 'eyes' to a position near the door. The other has a very distinctive grip at the end to distinguish it from the safelight cord or is also taken to another point in the room.

Ample storage space is available under the benches, protected by sliding doors fitted to the front.

Construction, Electrics and Plumbing

Setting up your own darkroom from scratch calls for various skills, ie, woodworking, electrical installation and plumbing. Be not afraid, however. The simple hand saw, hammer and nail, a modicum of determination and a chapter such as this by one who has suffered as you will, can help you much more than you think.

Cladding the walls

An outside location in garage or shed is likely to need wall cladding. Timber constructions are relatively weatherproof in the ordinary sense of the word but they provide very little insulation against cold and damp. They are usually about the easiest to clad because they are often erected on a framework to which sheets of hardboard can easily be pinned.

It may be sufficient to clad such a structure all round including the roof area, but it is preferable to insulate the gap behind the hardboard. There are various ways of doing this—using metal foil, expanded polystyrene in sheets or granules, glass fibre, mineral wool and so on. Any of the materials recommended for insulating roof spaces will do. Rolls of glass fibre are perhaps the easiest to use but wear garden or industrial gloves when you handle this material. It can be very irritating to the hands. Use a thickness of at least 60 mm, preferably more, but do not compress it. It relies for its effect on the air trapped in it.

If it is not practical to pack thick material behind the cladding, metal foil or heavy duty plastic sheeting might be used instead. At worst, you might at least keep the damp out by covering the rear of the cladding with a bitumen-based paint.

Hardboard is the cheapest cladding but more protection is offered by insulating board, which is softer, much thicker and about twice as expensive. Both are supplied in standard 8 × 4 foot panels.

Fastening the cladding to the wall is easy if you have a timber framework. Panel pins or hardboard pins are easily obtainable but for insulating board you need special large-headed nails. It is worth getting a panel-pin pusher for this job—a gadget that enables you to push the pins into the hardboard via a spring-loaded plunger in a thin tube. Hardboard is tough and it is not easy to hammer small pins into it.

If you have no timber framework, as in a concrete garage, you have to build one to fix the cladding to. With some structures, this is quite a problem because you cannot easily drill into concrete and it is at this stage that you might consider a timber floor. We dealt with this in the previous chapter from the insulation viewpoint but it can also help to provide an anchoring for your framework and for a partition if you are allowed only part of the garage.

Your framework should be made from timber at least 25 × 40 mm (1 × 1½ inches) simply constructed with top and bottom rungs, and uprights at 60 cm (2 foot) separation. If you cannot fix it to the wall, you must rely on force-fitting from side to side, top to bottom and/or end to end.

You can, of course, leave your outside location unclad and rely on such heating as you are able to provide but concrete, in particular, is very cold indeed and your heating bill may be enormous. Moreover, you generally need some timber to put in shelves, electricity points, switches, etc.

Even when you finish the wall cladding, you are likely to have a lot of gaps to fill up. Corrugated roofing material, for example, commonly leaves large gaps through which light and air stream unhindered. The garage manufacturers often supply eaves-filling kits as a remedy but if you do not have such a kit you will have to plug the gaps as best you can. The handyman skilled with a jig-saw can cut pieces of timber to a suitable shape. You and I, perhaps, are reduced to stuffing them with glass fibre wool, plastic foam or whatever comes handy.

Making the workbenches

Working surfaces are most suitably fastened to the wall if possible because that helps to keep them upright and avoids the problem of getting all the legs the same size. Plugging to the wall, however, does imply a degree of permanence and entails boring holes in the wall, which may not always be acceptable.

Walls vary in construction. The traditional brick wall with plaster covering is relatively easy to drill, but you can never be sure what is under the plaster. In surprisingly many houses, the quality of the bricks leaves something to be desired. Breeze blocks (black, cinder-like texture) give no trouble but if the wall is simply a lath and plaster construction, leave it well alone.

Provided your wall is suitable, the rear support for the bench is a wooden batten about 25 × 75 or 100 mm (1 × 3 or 4 inches). Such a relatively thin batten is much easier to fix than the 50 × 50 mm material often recommended. Drill holes about 60 cm (2 feet) apart along the length of the batten to take about a No 10 screw that will project at least 20 mm ($\frac{3}{4}$ inch) into the wall. Of course, if you have just put up a partition, or clad your walls for insulation, you will know exactly where the battens are. Then you can screw your fittings directly to them.

Hold the batten in the desired position on the wall (about 80 cm or 32 inches from the floor). You will need help if it is a long bench and, preferably, a spirit level. Otherwise, measure up from the floor at each end to make sure you get it straight. It is not a bad idea to mark the wall all round the ends of the batten at this stage so that you can return it to the same position later. Hold the batten securely in position and mark the wall clearly through the centres of the screw holes, preferably with a spike. Put the batten aside and, with the correct size masonry drill (for the size of screw you use) drill the wall carefully to a fraction more than the depth required. Make the holes in exactly the right position. If you use an electric drill, push the drill bit hard into the wall before switching it on and set it to the lowest speed. Plug the holes with proprietary wall plugs if they are clean and cylindrical. If the holes tend to be ragged, use the wall-plug substitute—a loose fibrous material that you damp before pushing it into the hole with the tool provided. Do not overmoisten this material. If you do, let it dry out a little before the next step. Take the batten to the wall again and position it carefully. Screw it to the wall securely but do not overtighten the screws. If they feel very loose, you have the wrong wall plug, the wall has crumbled or your loose filling is too loose. You will have to make another hole and try again.

When you have finished, take hold of the centre of the batten with both hands and pull outwards hard. It should be impossible to move it. If it comes out, bringing large lumps of plaster with it, your screws were not long enough or the wall is a bad one and you had better forget about plugging to it and go for a free-standing unit.

Some people have the confidence to hammer a batten on to the wall with masonry nails—very tough nails specially made for the purpose. It might work if you care to take the risk. A batten properly screwed to the wall will never come off.

We have spent a little time on this part of the construction because it is rather important. The rest of the woodwork is relatively simple and can be readily understood from diagrams. Hammer and nails, with occasional screws are generally all that are necessary. The true handyman will make neat joints and always use screws. Your general rule can be that a screw is unnecessary when a nail will go in. Clumsy joints are mostly out of sight and those that are not can be covered.

Nails have two main problems. First, whatever you nail into must be firmly supported; otherwise the hammer just bounces off; and in the end you split the wood. Secondly, they can be pulled out relatively easily. Knowing these limitations, you can quite easily get round them.

A batten on the wall provides firm support all along the rear of the bench. All you need then are cross pieces from the batten to the front legs and a long, deepish front piece nailed to the front of the legs. The diagram opposite shows the principle. If you use the wood-block method of securing the cross pieces to the rear batten, nail the blocks to the side pieces before securing them to the rear batten—unless you use screws in pre-drilled holes for this job. You should always put screws into pre-drilled holes but in softwood (and that is what you should be using) it is often possible to belt them in most of the way with a hammer and use the screwdriver for the last few turns.

The legs need be no sturdier than 50 mm square (2 × 2 inches). There is no harm in putting in more strength but timber is very

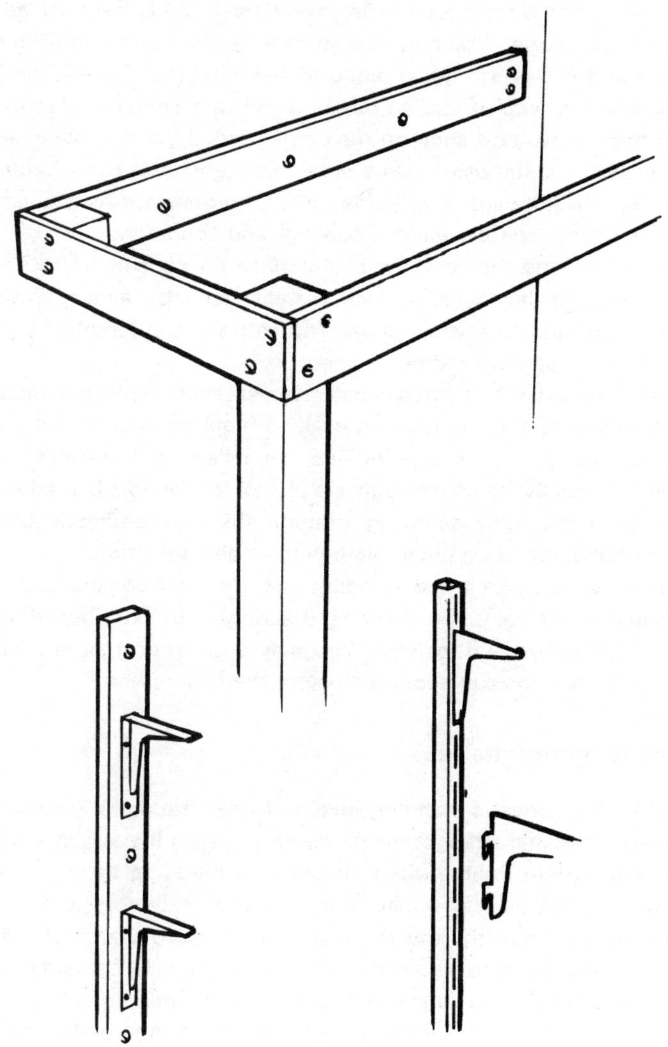

The bench support *(top)* depends largely on the strength of the wall fixing and the weight of the top. For extra rigidity, fasten the legs to the floor with angle irons, or increase the depth of the side and front battens.
Shelf brackets can be fastened to timber battens or you can use one of the commercial slotted systems.

expensive. You do not have to use new timber. Study the small ads in your local paper. You may find somebody offering second-hand timber and it is worth going along to see what they have. Take a steel rule with you. If you do buy new, go to a timber yard rather than the handyman's shop on the corner and, if you see materials advertised at a surprisingly low price, have a look at them before you buy. Hardboard and some of the proprietary laminated-surface boards come in various qualities and conditions.

If you can stand the cost, the best surface for your bench is undoubtedly the laminated-surface material sold by almost every timber yard and handyman shop. You can get it in lengths up to 8 feet and in various widths.

If that is too expensive you can use materials such as blockboard or old floorboards and surface it yourself with plastic floorcovering or similar material. Planks or boards can be nailed on. The laminated board is usually heavy enough simply to lay on top but added security is given by screwing through the top (definitely pre-drilled holes) or fixing underneath with small angle irons.

If you have to make a free-standing unit, the front construction is repeated at the back. If it is not rigid enough, put extra horizontal struts part way down the legs. You may wish to do that anyway because the struts can support a useful shelf.

Putting up the shelves

This is now almost a standing joke, but there are many shelf kits available that make the job relatively easy—again if you can stand the cost. Where trouble often occurs is in plugging the required support to the wall. The ostensibly simplest method is to screw shelf brackets directly into the wall. With a good wall that may work but it is easier to plug vertical battens to the wall first and then fasten the brackets to them, especially if you are putting up a bank of several shelves. This is the principle of the slotted metal strips into which brackets are inserted as required. It is easier and the finished job is stronger when the component plugged to the wall has very little depth.

It might appear that a bracket has no depth but the top screw does, in fact, take quite a strain and the wall plugging often cannot withstand it. A much shorter screw into wood can take a much greater strain that is not directly transmitted to a single screw in the wall. The metal strips of the shelving kits can be so securely fastened to the wall that their shelves can take an incredible weight. Look for the sturdier types, however, that allow the brackets to be screwed to the shelves or the semi-industrial type with U-section brackets.

Putting in the power

One thing you must have in your darkroom is electricity and it is virtually essential that you provide yourself with several separate outlets. Adaptors and trailing cables plugged into one socket are inconvenient, untidy and potentially dangerous.

In this section, we must inevitably deal with United Kingdom type electricity supplies and regulations. The principles may be common to many countries but there are others (notably the United States) using a different voltage and different connectors. Regulations undoubtedly vary from country to country and there are those in which no wiring can be carried out by the householder. In the UK, there are no such regulations but any new installation or modification should be inspected by the appropriate electricity board.

In the UK, the supply voltage is 240, which simply means that your equipment must be designed for use on a 240-volt supply, either direct or through a transformer. Most projectors and some enlargers use low-voltage (about 12-volt) lamps and must be connected through a transformer, which is a device for converting the supply from one voltage to another (generally lower). The transformer is often built into projectors but may be a separate item for enlargers.

How we get electricity

The electricity arrives at your house in two very thick cables—black and red—that are connected via a heavy-duty electricity board fuse to your fusebox or domestic consumer unit. There the supply is split up via smaller fuses which connect thinner cables to your outlets—wall sockets for power supplies and ceiling or other connectors for lights. In the ring main circuit now generally installed, the power fuses are rated at 30 amps and the lighting fuses at 5 amps.

An amp or ampere is a unit of current flow. Whenever you connect an appliance to an electricity supply, it consumes electricity which flows (for want of a better word) along the cables. The rate of that flow is measured in amps and is governed by the power requirement or consumption of the appliance. The consumption of power is measured in watts. An electric heating appliance, for example, may need to consume 1,000 watts or 1 kW. To do that, it must cause current to flow at a rate calculated by dividing the rated wattage by the supply voltage, ie, in this case, 1,000/240 = 4.17 amps.

Two such fires would draw 8.32 amps and if they were plugged into a lighting circuit they would considerably overload the fuse, which should burn out. We shall continue to talk of fuses although many modern domestic consumer units are fitted with miniature contact breakers (MCBs) which cut off the supply when overloaded but can be reset merely by pressing a button—after you have removed the overload.

The prime function of the fuse or MCB is to stop the overload before it heats up the cables along which the electricity is supplied and causes a fire. The cables used for lighting circuits (they are often flexes rather than cables) can carry about six amps safely. The power cable (a true cable with heavy insulation and much less flexible) can carry about 21 amps but in modern installations is connected in an unbroken ring from a fuse in the consumer unit through various outlets and back to the same fuse. Each socket is therefore effectively supplied through two cables and such are the vagaries of electricity that although the same voltage is present in both cables, the current divides between the two. The cables could therefore carry about 42 amps between them without overheating but the fuse is rated at 30 amps for safety. That is ample for most domestic installations. The exceptions are electric cookers, and sometimes other highly-rated items such as immersion heaters. These are connected to separate circuits with their own fuses and suitably-rated flex.

Thus, each ring (and a house may well have two—one upstairs and one down) can carry 30 × 240 = 7,200 watts or 7.2 kW. You must not, however, connect all that load to one socket because the contacts in the socket can carry safely only about 13 amps or 3.2 kW. Consequently, the plug on the appliance (the three flat pin type) also carries a fuse with a maximum rating of 13 amps. The prime function of this fuse, however, is to protect the appliance. The current-carrying leads into the appliance are red and black in the case of cables and brown and black in the case of flexes. Most appliances have flexes, in which the wires are stranded. In cables, the wires (or conductors) are much thicker single strand. The red or brown wire is 'live'; the black or blue is 'neutral'. This means that the live wire has the mains voltage on it in respect to the voltage-less earth. If you connect a lamp between it and a good connection to the earth, the lamp will light. This is called a potential difference; the live wire has a potential difference in respect to earth of 240 volts, whereas the neutral wire is at the same (zero) potential as earth—or very nearly so in practice.

Why earthing is important

We said that the lamp lights if you connect it between the live wire and earth. So do you—almost. The human body is not quite as good a conductor of electricity as a metal wire but it does conduct. If you stand on a concrete floor with a live wire in your hand and somebody throws the switch, a heavy current will flow through your body and will amost certainly kill you. If you were on a wooden floor, you would feel the effect but you might get away with it. You will not normally grasp a live wire but you might well touch a faulty appliance in which the current has been allowed to reach the outer casing.

For that reason, the normal electrical cable has three wires—live, neutral and earth. In cables, the earth wire is unprotected inside the relatively thick outer insulation. In flexes, it has its own additional green-and-yellow striped insulation. These earth wires run from all outlets to the domestic consumer unit, where they are firmly attached to a good earth connection installed by the electricity board. The three-pin plug attached to the appliance carries a third wire to its largest pin to which all non-current-carrying metal parts, and particularly the outer case are connected.

Thus, if current is caused to flow through any of these parts it is immediately channelled to earth. As the earth wire makes a much better conductor than your body, you would probably feel little shock.
The efficiency of the earth wire as a conductor (it has virtually no resistance to the current, unlike most appliances) means that the current flow is huge. That is another electrical law: the lower the resistance to the flow of electricity, the greater the current. In practice, the flow is so great that the fuse is blown and the danger removed.
The 'short-circuit' caused by the fault might be caused by component failure, allowing the heavy current to flow through other components before reaching earth. That current might be enough to damage those components if it were prolonged. So the immediate cutout effected by the blown fuse protects the appliance. Some appliances are more easily damaged than others and, provided their current consumption is not too great, they can be protected by a smaller fuse. Consequently, plug fuses are available in standard ratings of 13 amps and 3 amps. Additionally, many items have fuses built in of a much lower rating—one amp or less.

Extending the supply

Again, we have to say that electricity board regulations require you to have any work you do on your fixed house wiring to be inspected before you start to use it. We must also say that, unless you are sure you understand exactly what you are doing, do not do it. Call in a qualified electrician.
Now we know how electricity comes into the house, we can think about extending it. Take the simplest case first. You are in a room that has a single socket and we want more in a more accessible place. There is one simple, inexpensive, legal and perfectly safe way of doing that. You buy an extension panel from almost any electrical or chain store. This is a single long, neat plastic housing with up to four sockets, a warning light and a fuse. You merely connect a flex of suitable length and a plug on the end of it and you have four more sockets anywhere you want them. You can even fix them to the wall—and you can completely isolate them when

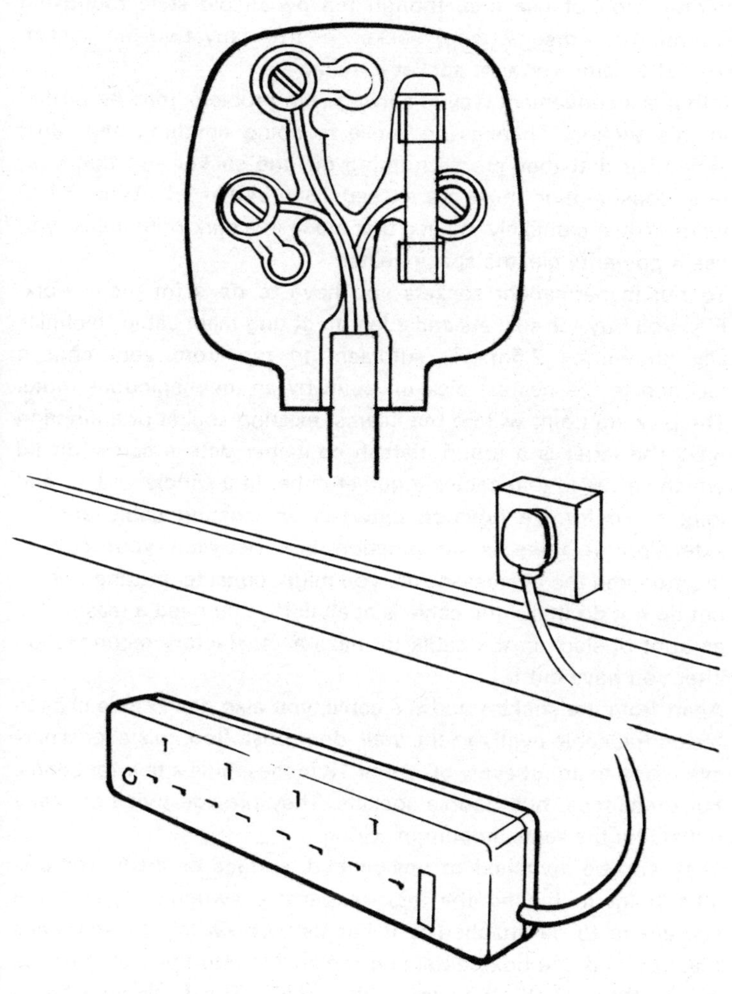

Wiring a 13 amp plug. The brown wire goes to the fuse, the green and yellow to the large flat pin and the blue to the other smaller pin.
Extension panels *(bottom)* are available from electrical shops and stores. All you have to do is fit a length of cable and a plug.

not in use by pulling out the plug. Such a solution does not require any approval because you are not altering any part of the fixed wiring. Do not use one, though fed by an old-style round-pin 5 amp (or, worse, 2 amp) socket, or from any two-pin socket. An old 15 amp (power) socket is suitable.

If that is a convenient way of solving your problem, read no further in this section. There is no sense in doing anything else. Just remember that they are all running off one socket and that your total consumption must not exceed 13 × 240 = 3.1 kW or 3,100 watts. You are unlikely to need that much in a darkroom unless you use a powerful electric space heater.

To put in permanent sockets you have to do a lot more work. First you buy the sockets and a length of ring main cable (technically known as 2.5 mm^2) sufficient to run from your chosen location to the nearest pick-up point by an inconspicuous route. The pick-up point will be the nearest existing socket or a junction box. The latter is a round, flattish container with a screw off lid which serves to join cables together either in a simple end-to-end joint or to form a junction between an existing cable and an extension. If there is no junction box between your chosen location and the nearest socket, you might consider putting one in, but do not do that if the cable is at all tight. You need a reasonable amount of slack in the cable to make a satisfactory reconnection after you have cut it.

Apart from the sockets and the cable, you also need cable clips to fasten the cable neatly to the wall, door post, floor joists, or whatever—one to about every 50 cm or 18 inches, plus a few for bends. For preference, buy double sockets. They provide twice as many outlets for the same amount of wiring.

They can be switched or unswitched, surface or flush. There is little point in buying the more expensive switched type if the equipment to be attached to it has its own switch. Flush means that you sink the box containing the socket into the wall. Surface means that you fix it to the wall surface. The flush type has a different box, generally metal and smaller than the outer panel. The surface type has a plastic box the same size as the front panel. It is much easier to handle because few walls now have plaster of such a depth that the box can be sunk into it. You usually have to

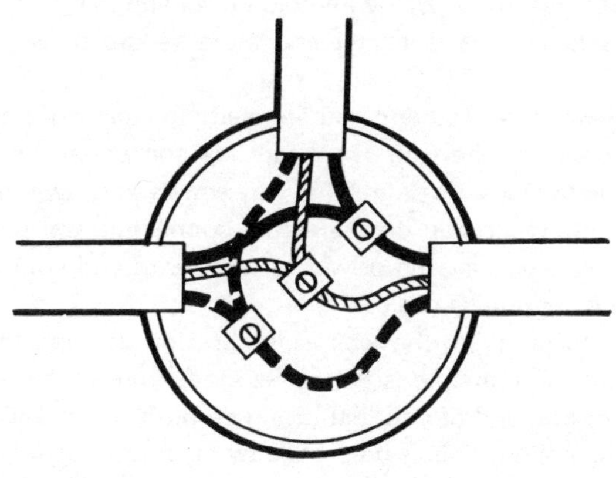

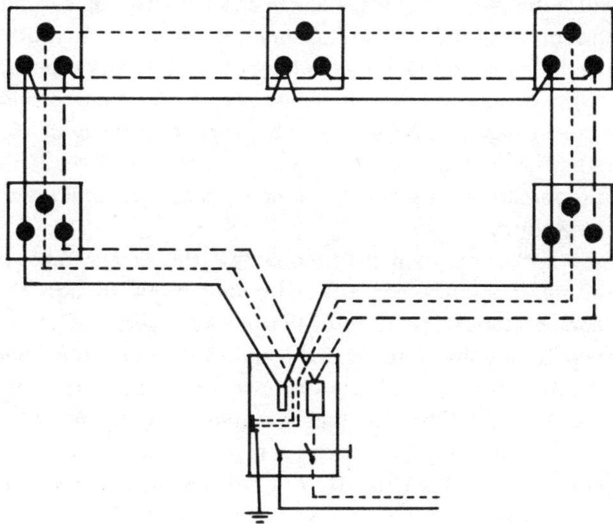

The junction box *(top)* allows the existing wiring to be tapped. All wires of the same colour go to the same terminal.
The principle of the ring main *(bottom)* is that a single cable runs from a fuse in the domestic consumer unit through all the sockets and back to the same fuse.

gouge a hole out of the wall with cold chisel and hammer. Nevertheless, the flush type is neater and more secure once properly fixed.

With all the materials to hand you are ready to start work. Start by fixing the boxes to the wall, then wire the sockets and carry the cable back to the pick-up point. That way you need to switch off the electricity only while you do the actual connecting up. If you go the other way, you have no power to work with and your electric drill, if you have one, is useless.

We dealt with plugging the wall in the section devoted to workbenches and the principle is the same. Once you have the boxes secured take one end of your cable and strip off about 100 mm of the outer insulation. This is best done by laying the cable flat and cutting down the middle—where the earth wire is—with a sharp thin blade. You will find various places in the box where you can knock out a hole for the cable entry. Choose the one most convenient for the way the cable is to run and feed the cable in. Pull it well through to give you room to carry out the wiring comfortably. Take the red cable to the L hole in the back of the socket plate, the black to the N hole and the bare wire to the E. Cut them to suitable lengths to lie reasonably flat behind the socket. Strip about 10 mm or $\frac{1}{4}$ inch off the black and red insulation, insert all three wires in their appropriate holes and tighten the grub screws until the wires are held securely.

Place the socket plate on the box, pulling the excess cable back through the hole in the box as you do so. Do not, though, let the black and red tapes come out of the box uncovered by the outer insulation. Screw the plate on to the box. Run your cable along its allotted route. If you have used a flush box that usually means cutting a channel in the wall plaster down or up as the case may be. Keep the cable taut and flat and secure it to the wall, door frame or whatever with cable clips. Do not run the cable through doorways or window openings. It may become damaged by the door or window, or by people walking through. Such an expedient is not approved by the regulations. From one room to another, you must pass the cable through (or under) the wall.

When you reach the pick-up point, turn off the electricity at the consumer point or pull out the fuse serving that particular circuit.

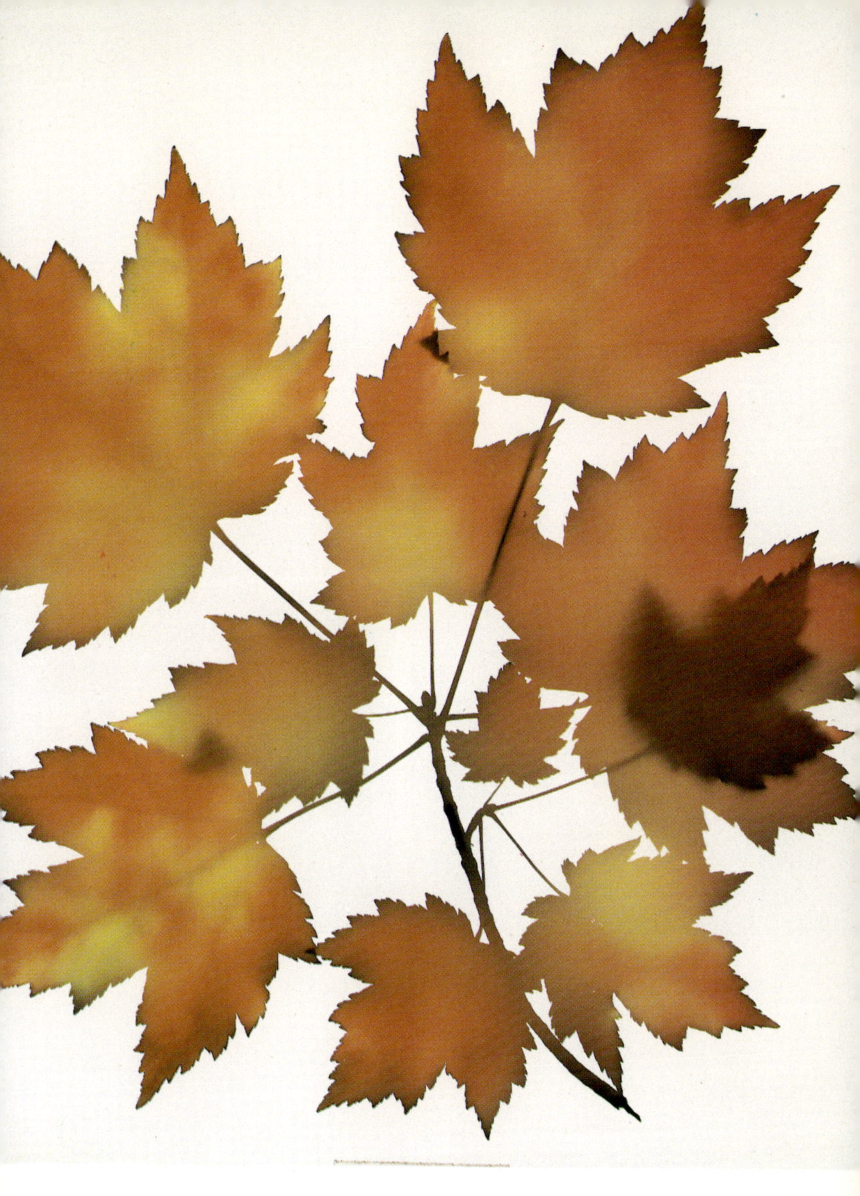

Reversal materials are ideal for making photograms in full colour. This picture was made simply by laying leaves on a sheet of Cibachrome A, and then processing it. *From The Focalguide to Cibachrome.*

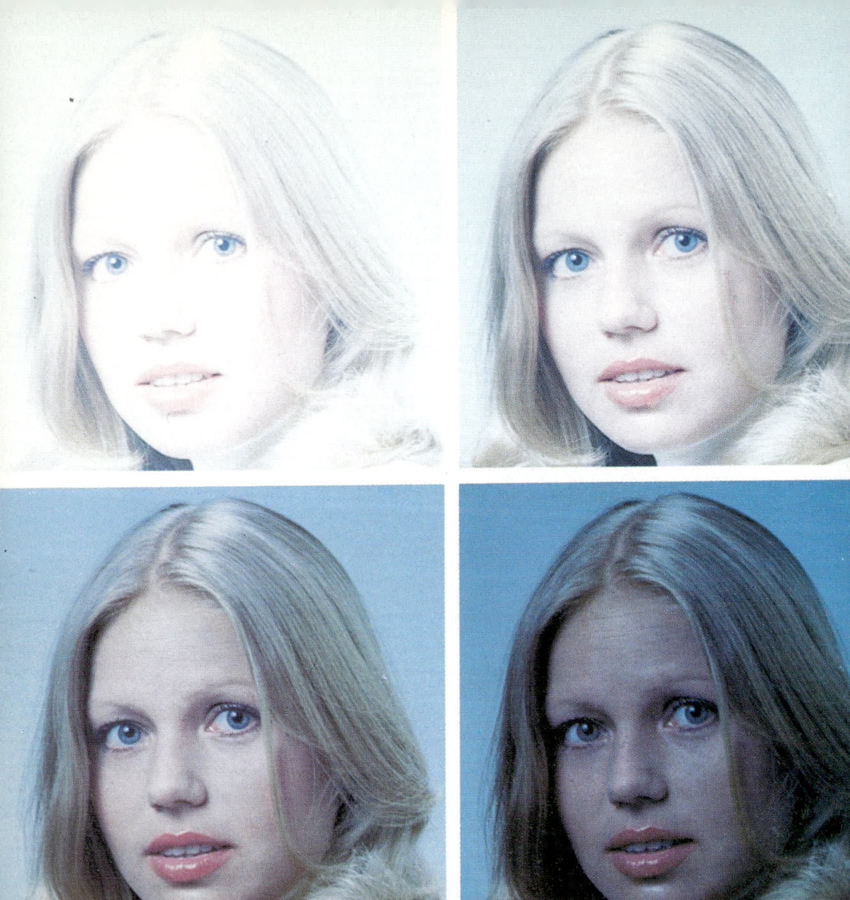

These four tests were expected to 'straddle' the correct exposure for the particular negative. The four exposure times were given 5, 10, 20 and 40 sec and the filtration was 120Y and 80M. From these tests it was estimated that a 13 sec exposure would give the correct density.

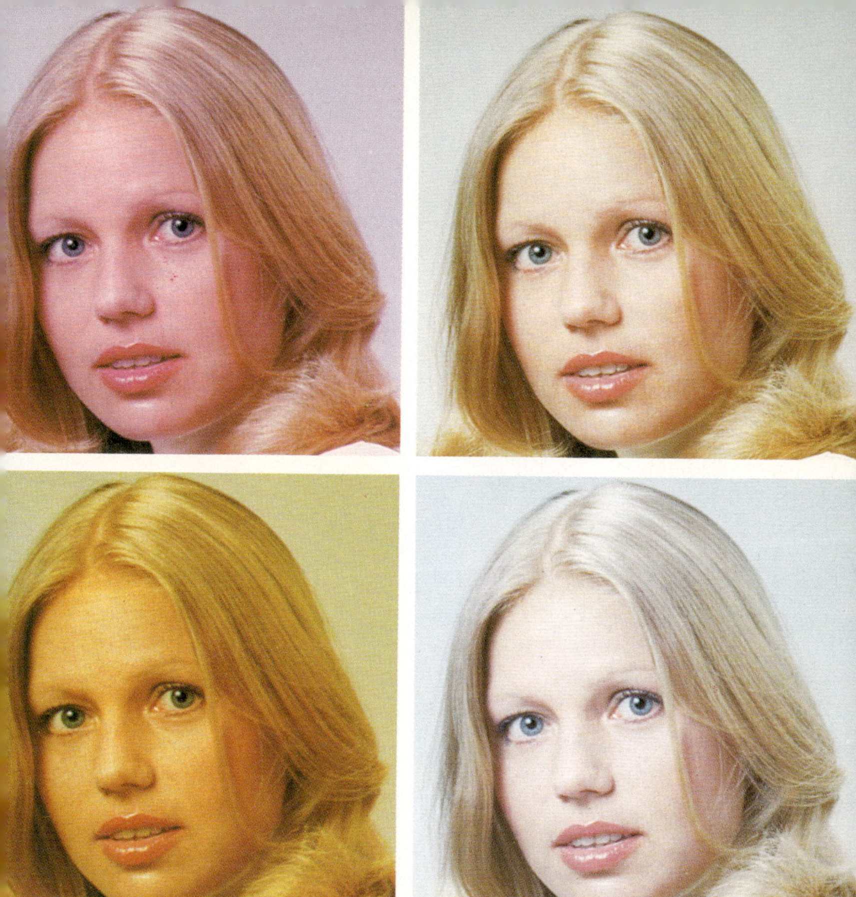

A colour test was then made, using these filters: 100Y and 50M (*top left*); 100Y and 70M (*top right*); 80Y and 70M (*bottom left*); 110Y and 80M (*bottom right*). All four exposures were for 13 sec. *From The Focalguide to Colour Printing from Negatives and Slides.*

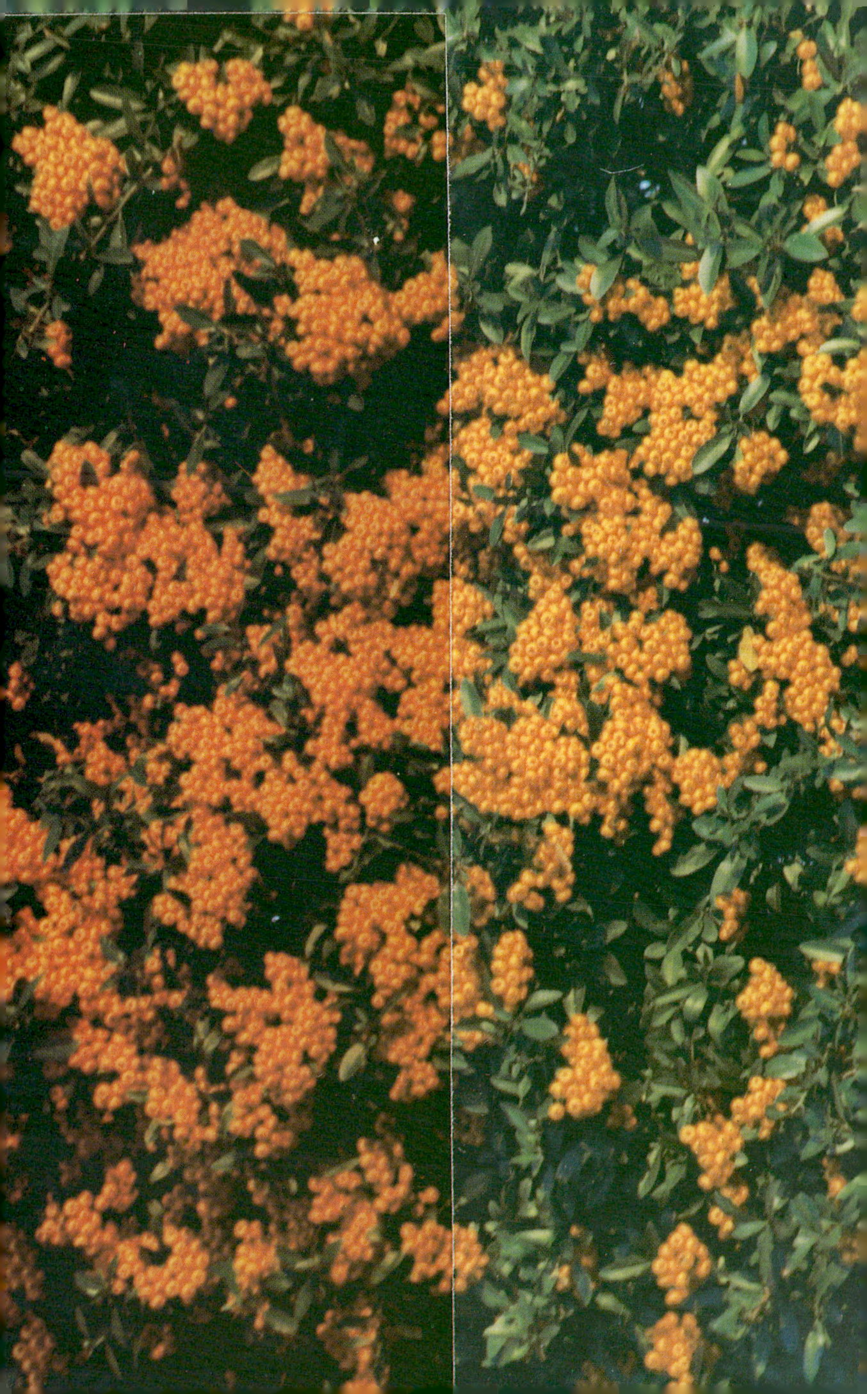

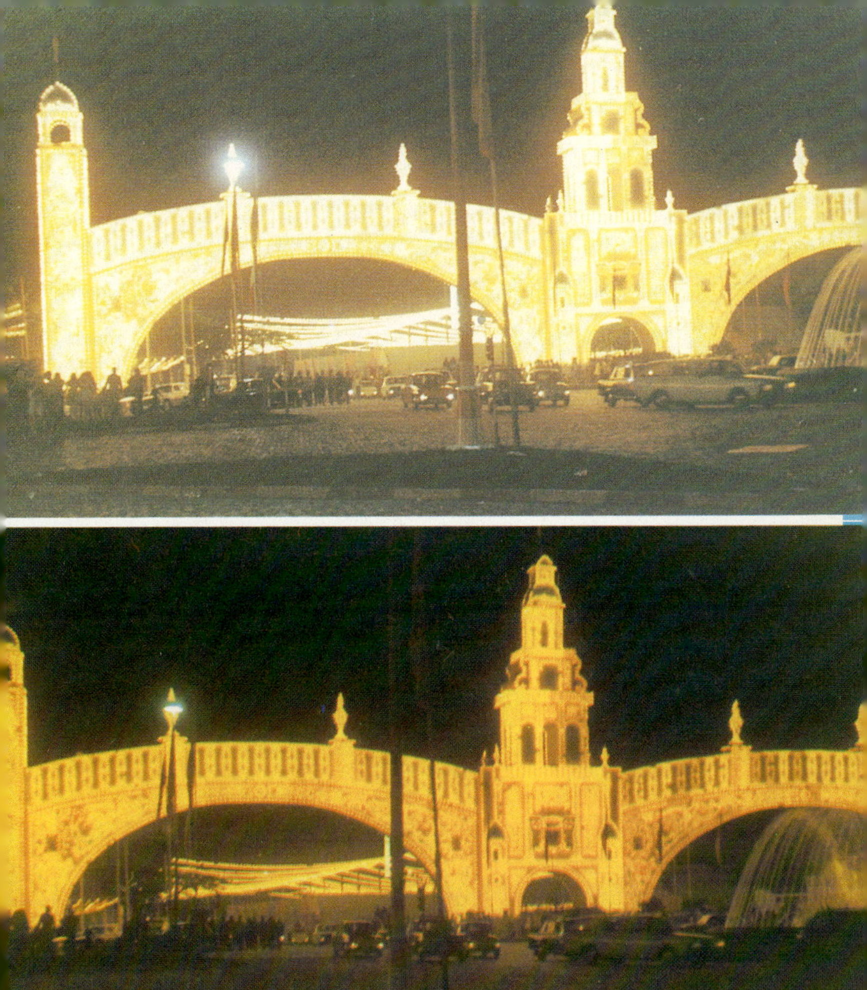

Making your own prints lets you choose how a picture should look. With an unusual negative, you often get a poor print from a commercial develop and print service (*top*). It is easy to do much better yourself (*bottom*). *Clyde Reynolds.*

Opposite: When you print your own pictures, you can choose the colours that you like best. *Clyde Reynolds.*

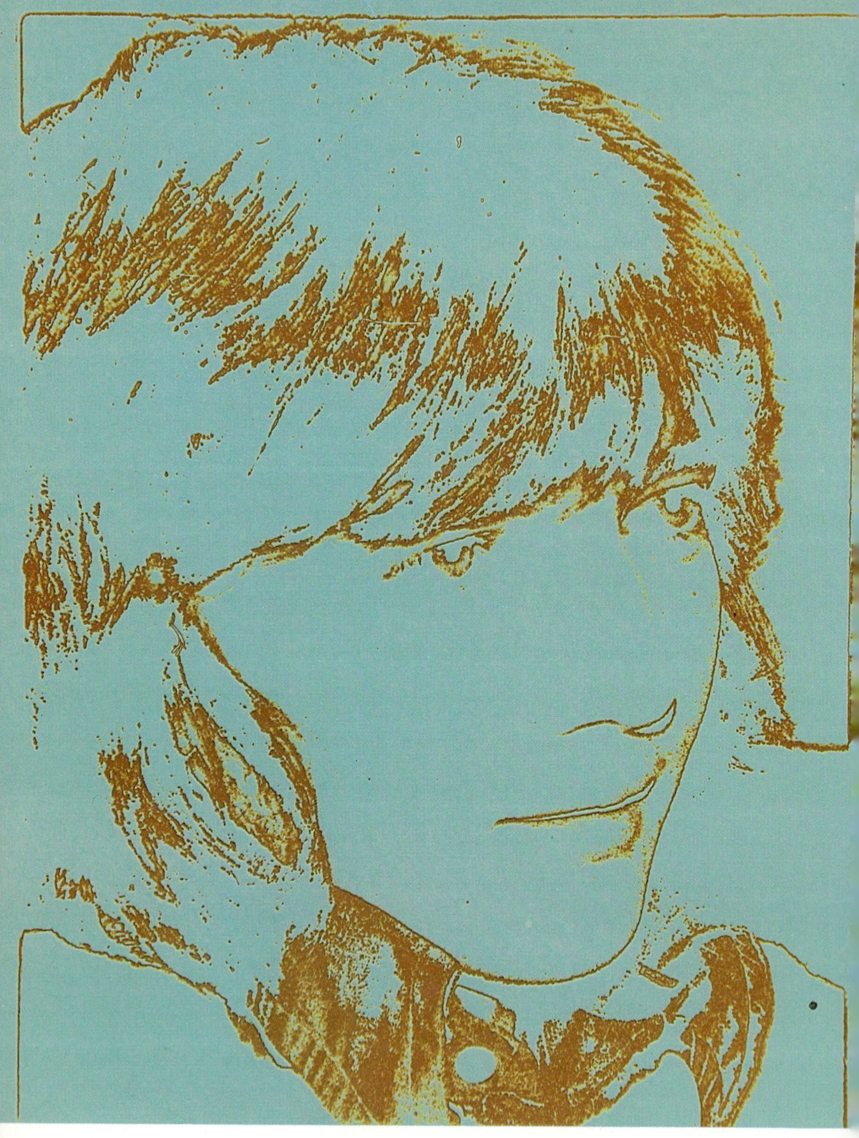

You can make colour prints from black-and-white negatives. Colour paper was exposed by strong cyan light to a black-and-white solarised negative. The paper was then fogged with a normal bromide paper safelight providing a cyan coloured background. *Leonard Gaunt.*

Opposite: Coloured-base papers provide a simple way of providing coloured pictures. You can paste together parts of two identical prints to produce this effect.

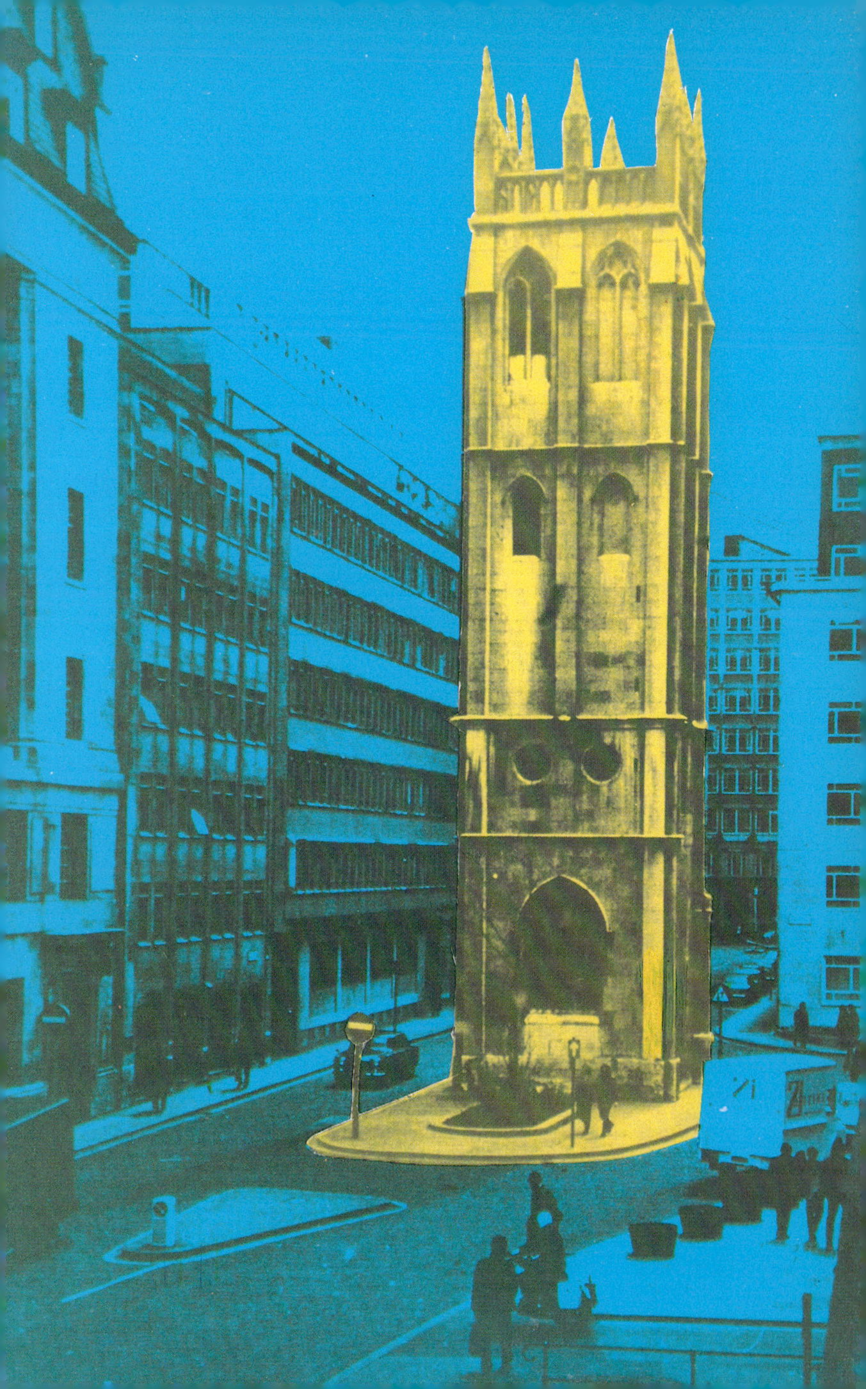

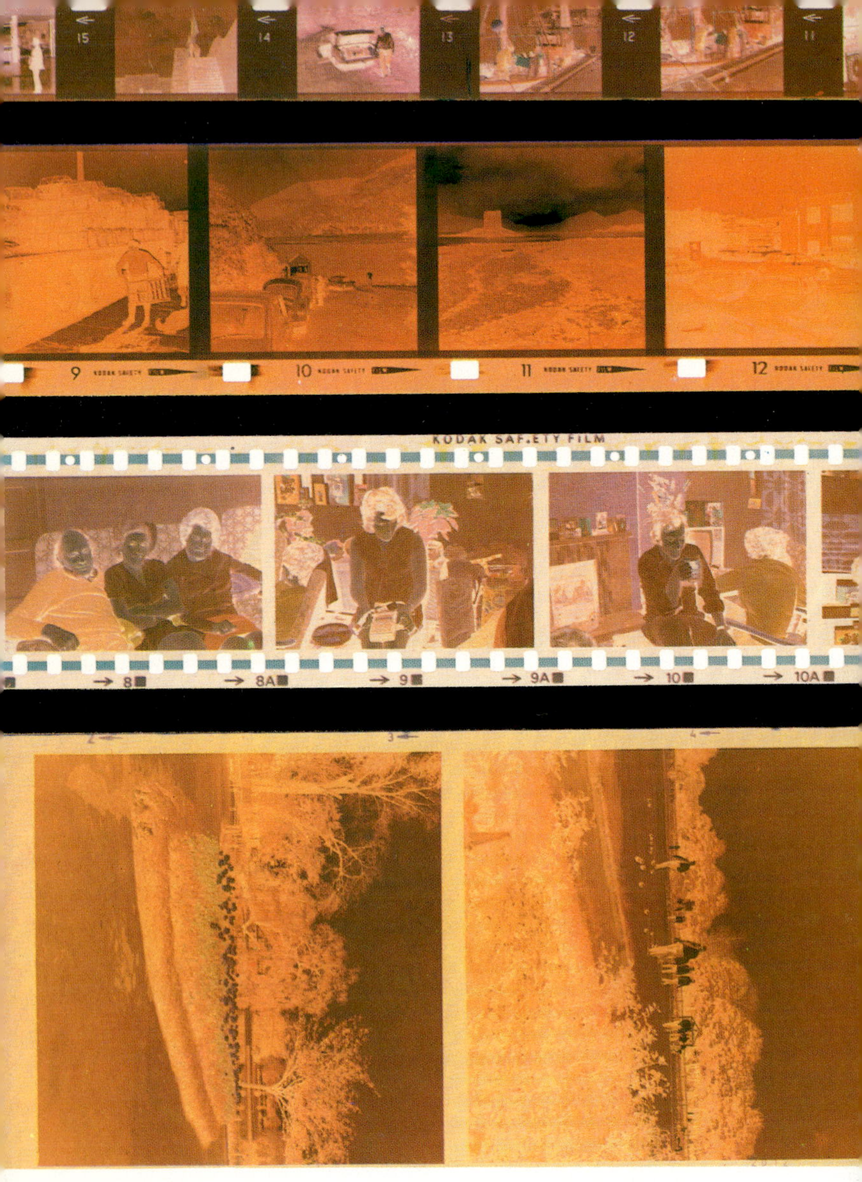

Some colour negative types and formats. *From top to bottom* 110 Kodacolor II, 126 Kodacolor X, 35 mm Kodacolor II, 120 (6 x 6 cm) Agfacolor CNS. *From The Focalguide to Colour Printing from Negatives and Slides.*

Return to the pick-up point and unscrew the socket plate from its box. Pull the plate clear of the box. It should bring a short length of cable with it—or two lengths if it is part of a ring main. All you have to do now is to feed your cable into the box (which may entail removing the box if it is a flush type) and connect it in exactly the same way as you did the other socket. You should then have two or three wires at each terminal. Make sure that all wires are securely held by the grub screws. Replace the socket plate and you are finished—apart from switching on again at the consumer unit.

Observing the regulations

There are regulations, of course. The additional wiring we have just described is known as a spur. The regulations say that you must not have more spurs on a ring main than the socket outlets on the ring. That need not concern us too much but the regulations add that not more than two sockets (or one double socket) can be connected to each spur, which is awkward if you intended to connect four. If it were not for this regulation, you could just add two further sockets by wiring another double socket to the one you have just installed. All you need is a short length of cable to connect red to red, black to black and earth (bare wire) to earth.

To keep within the regulations, however, you should run two separate spurs from your original socket or you should extract one set of wires from that socket and take it to a junction box. You then run one set of wires from the new double socket to the junction box and another set to the old socket. You have then, in effect, extended the ring and can run a spur from the new double socket to serve another pair.

An odd point about the regulations is that you can connect your spur circuit to the original socket via a plug instead of wiring it in. It is then a temporary supply and is within the regulations.

Wiring outside locations

If your garage or other outbuilding already has an approved electricity supply you can proceed in the way we have just described, bearing in mind, perhaps, that the supply may already be a spur and is subject to the regulations regarding the number of sockets.

If the location has no supply, you have to take it from the house. The procedure is broadly the same but you cannot, according to the regulations, connect to the ring main unless the location is attached to the house. If it is a detached structure, your final connection must be made to a separate fuse at the main fuse box or domestic consumer unit. Moreover, you must take the supply into the outbuilding via an isolating switch. The normal switch is in the live wire only: it does not break the neutral wire. An isolating switch breaks both wires and disconnects the outside wiring totally from the main supply.

There is more! If you run the cable underground, it must be at least 50 cm (18 inches) down and enclosed in heavy gauge galvanized steel conduit—or you can use special underground cable. If it runs overground, it must be suspended from a strainer (stranded galvanized wire) at least 3.5 m (12 feet) above the ground and attached to it at intervals of no more than 30 cm (12 inches). You can omit the straining wire if the run is no more than 3 m (10 feet). Alternatively you can run it along a wall provided it is enclosed in heavy gauge galvanized steel conduit but you must not run it along a fence.

Safety is particularly important with outside locations, where the risk of electrical shock is greater. When you run a cable into a building, make sure that the entry is completely watertight. Secure the cable just outside the building so that the entry is in an upward direction. Water cannot then run down the cable to an inside connector.

If you are in any doubt at all—as with any other electrical wiring—do not do it!

Lamps and lighting

Safelights and white lights can be plugged into any available socket (with a 3 amp fuse in the plug) or they can be wired separately. Regulations now demand that lighting circuits also

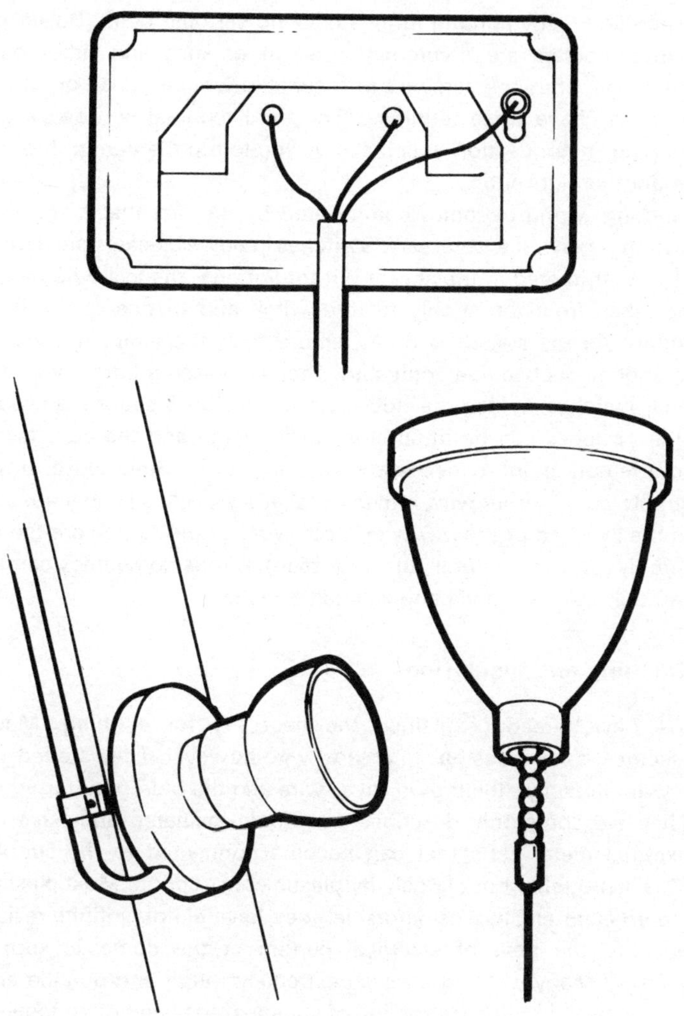

The double socket has internal connections and therefore needs only three terminals to accept the live, neutral and earth wires.
Pull switches *(right)* are advisable and sometimes obligatory in the presence of water.
Batten lampholders *(left)* are simply screwed to any available surface at any required angle.

carry an earth wire although most houses are probably not so wired and many lighting fittings have no earthing point. So-called batten holders are commonly used in garages and other outbuildings. They are screwed to a suitable wooden base or batten and may have three terminals. The third terminal is, however, a looping-in connection which allows you to run the wiring through to another light fitting.

Lighting wiring becomes complicated by the fact that a separate switch is generally necessary. Switches in power sockets are generally incorporated in the socket but for lighting, the live wire has to be taken from the supply to the switch and thence to the light fitting. As the switch is often remote from the lamp, the wiring arrangements become confusing. They are eased a little if you use pull switches, which are advisable in outside locations anyway. Pull switches can be fitted close to the lamp and the cord taken to a remote point as necessary. Or they can be fitted close to the supply point. Either way, remember that a switch is simply a break in the live (red or brown) wire. Both wires at the switch are therefore live but the neutral (black or blue) wire is sometimes carried through the switch via an insulated terminal.

Earthing and insulation

We have already explained the necessity for earthing. Many electrical appliances have no earth wire however. They are fed via a twin flex only—the brown (live) wire and the blue (neutral) wire. They are commonly described as double-insulated and have no external metal parts that can become connected to the supply. This is brought about largely by plastic construction. Most plastics are efficient electric insulators, ie, they have almost infinite resistance to the flow of electrical current at the domestic supply voltage. Many of them are also extremely tough and durable and can be used in the construction of spindles, cogs and other moving parts that previously had to be made from metal. Where metal still has to be used, therefore, it can be effectively isolated from the electrical conductors by connecting it through plastic components. Such appliances are generally of relatively low power ie, they draw little current. Anything drawing in excess of one amp or so is likely to be fed by three wires–commonly called twin and earth. In that case it is vital that the earth wire (green and yellow) is connected to the main earth via the large pin of the three-pin plug. This is for your own safety. Unearthed equipment is dangerous!

Water and plumbing

We explained at the beginning of this book that running water is by no means a necessity in a darkroom. If you have a reasonably large, permanent darkroom, however, and particularly if it is isolated from the house, running water is certainly convenient.

To install it you have to know something about plumbing. Modern plumbing is effected by relatively small bore copper tubing that is remarkably easy to use. With any luck you have such a pipe running to the cold water tap in your kitchen, probably of 15 mm tubing. You take your supply from this by cutting the pipe, fitting in a tee-junction and running another pipe out. It is almost as simple as it sounds.

In practice, you first turn off the water at the main stopcock and turn on the tap in case there is still any water under pressure in the pipe. You may have a drain cock that allows you to drain away any remaining water in the pipe rising to the tap. If not some water will escape when you cut the pipe.

Make an absolutely square cut (with a sharp hacksaw blade) in the pipe at about 60 cm (2 feet) from floor level. Take a compression tee-junction (see later) and fit it into the pipe. This entails making a further cut to remove a small piece of the pipe. Tighten the nuts hard. Fit about 15-30 cm (6 to 12 inches) of new pipe into the tee and fit a screw-down stopcock (also see later) to the other end with the arrow on its body pointing in the direction of the water flow. Again, tighten the nuts hard. Turn off the new stopcock, turn on the main stopcock and the household water supply is restored. The rest of the work can be carried out at your convenience. The stopcock is put in here so that you can cut off the darkroom supply when it is not required–especially necessary in the case of an outside darkroom where the pipe may be subjected to freezing temperatures.

Materials and fittings

While we are awaiting your convenience let us consider the materials. The 15 mm tubing is supplied in 3-metre lengths and is easily bent by hand provided you use a bending spring for all but the most gradual bends. It can be joined with compression joints or capillary joints. A compression joint is fitted with nuts that you remove to reveal an olive or compression ring that fits over the tubing. In practice, you need only loosen the nut and push the pipe in through the ring until it reaches a stop. Tighten the nut and the soft copper ring is squeezed between tubing and nut, forming a perfect joint. You need to hold the tube in a wrench and tighten the nut with a spanner. Some say do not tighten it too hard and, if you ever need to undo the joint, it will retighten satisfactorily. Whether that is good advice is open to doubt.

Capillary joints need a blow lamp but they are neater and less expensive. They have an internal ring of solder in a recess around the tube. You push the tube into the joint and direct a blowlamp on to it until solder oozes out all round the joint. Wipe off the excess and you have a neat joint. Preparation has to be more careful for this type of joint. You must clean the end of the tubing thoroughly with steel wool and smear a little flux on to it before making the joint. You must make all joints together because the solder rings all melt when you apply heat to any part of the fitting. When making a joint in a pipe against a wall or other surface, slip a piece of asbestos behind the joint to protect the wall from the blowlamp flame.

Both types of joint are supplied in various shapes and sizes for making junctions or bends or simply for joining one length of pipe to another. They are also available with unequal outlets to allow different sizes of pipe to be joined. You would need such a joint, for example, to take a 15 mm supply from a 25 mm pipe.

There are various types of what we commonly call taps, too. You may not immediately recognize the description 'screw-down stopcock' but it is only another name for the type of valve that is inserted in a pipe to allow the supply to be turned off. It looks much like any other brass tap except that it has no spout. It always has an arrow engraved on its body to indicate the direction of the water

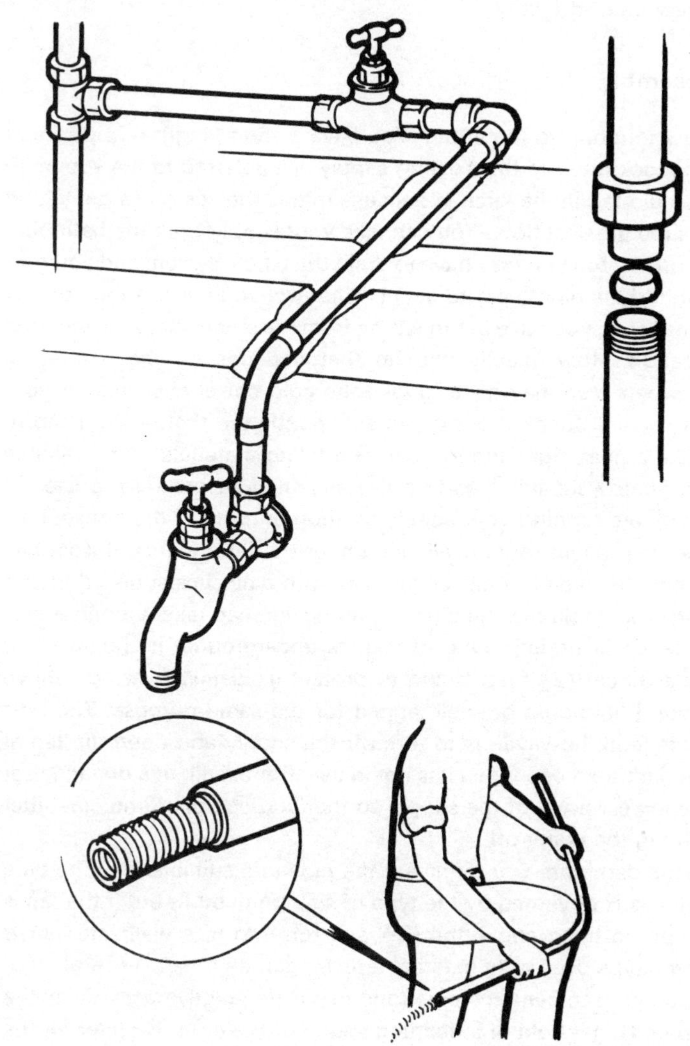

It is a relatively easy matter to fit an outside tap with the compression joints shown right. The text gives full details. If you have to bend the pipe, a bending spring stops it kinking.

flow and should always be inserted with the arrow pointing in the direction of the flow.

Assembly

Now to return to the fitting. You have a short length of pipe and a stopcock fitted to the existing supply. We referred to the supply to the cold tap in the kitchen because that is the easiest to get at and has the greatest flow. You can take your supply from the bathroom if you like but you may have to drain the whole system and you may not find the pipes easy to get at. Wherever you are, with the supply connected, you have to run tubing from the stopcock to the required location. How exactly you do that depends on the barriers in between. You may have to take the cold chisel and hammer to a wall again. Knock it out reasonably gently but there is no need to make a neat, tight-fitting hole. The filling materials now available from hardware stores and do-it-yourself shops are easy to use.

If you are running your supply to another room in the house, take the most direct route available, under the floorboards, if possible. Secure the pipe liberally all the way with pipe clips supplied for the purpose. If you run the pipe outdoors, you can take it along a wall or fence or underground. If it goes underground, it should be at least 80 cm ($2\frac{1}{2}$ feet) down to protect it against freezing. Above ground, it should be well lagged for the same purpose. The best protection, however, is to turn off the supply and open the tap at the darkroom end when it is not in use. Better still, fit a draincock at the lowest point of the supply so that you can drain the pipe after turning the water off.

In the darkroom you terminate the pipe in a suitable tap. The type you use is governed by the type of sink unit you fit but if the tap is simply to hang above the sink and run into it, a wallplate elbow of the type used to fit external taps for garden hoses is useful.

If you have to bend the pipe (and that is frequently necessary at the tap end), get hold of a bending spring of the right diameter for the pipe. Grease it slightly and insert it in the pipe to beyond the point of the bend. You can then easily bend the pipe over your knee without kinking it. To make removal of the spring easier, it is best to overbend and then ease back to the curve required. Insert a screwdriver through the ring at the end of the spring, twist anticlockwise and pull the spring free.

You can run hot water to your darkroom in the same way, of course, but a better idea, especially outdoors, might be to fit a small electric or gas heater connected into the supply. There are butane gas types that can be run from the same cylinder as a space heater if that is your choice.

Waste disposal and drainage

If you have running water in your darkroom, you need some method of running it out again. The easiest method is simply to fit a flexible hose or piece of polythene tubing to the outlet and run the waste into a suitable container under the bench. There are plenty of 20-litre or 4-5 gallon water carriers available that do the job admirably. You can even seal the tubing through the stopper to avoid fumes or overflow.

Plumbed-in drainage can be awkward. There are regulations about it, especially in newer buildings with single-stack drainage, ie, where all soil and waste runs into one main drainage pipe. If you can easily cut straight through a wall to a nearby existing gully, you should have little trouble because plastic piping and fittings can be used throughout and are quite easy to work with.

Draining an outside location could be effected by means of a soakaway but it means a lot of hard work. You have to dig a pit 1.5 m (5 feet) square and 1.5 m deep, 5 m from the building (and the house). You then fill it to about 30 cm (1 foot) from the top with rubble (broken bricks, stones, etc.) and run an underground soil pipe from the middle of the pit back to a gulley outside the darkroom into which the waste is discharged. Put the topsoil back over the rubble and your soakaway is operational.

All fittings are again plastic and are joined simply by pushing together through O-rings. The underground pipe is immensely strong but is easily cut with a hacksaw or any type of handyman's multi-purpose saw.

Keeping it warm

If your darkroom is inside the house, heating may be already available but you still have to consider its suitability. Any kind of non-radiant heating is fine but most gas fires and many electric heaters are of the radiant type: they emit light. You may be able to shield your working area from the glow, but it is not easy, particularly when loading films into developing tanks.

The ideal temperature you should aim at is about 21°C (70°F), which avoids in most cases any need for a dishwarmer to keep your developer at the correct temperature. Indoors, that should not be too difficult. Outdoors, it might be expensive if you have not insulated the darkroom carefully. It is best to avoid electrical heating unless you are certain that it will not overload your circuit. If you have, as you should have, a completely separate circuit from the consumer unit to your outside darkroom, you should have no problems with electric heating. Otherwise, when you turn on your 2 kW or more heater while other heavy demands are being made on the current in the house, you might well blow a fuse.

Other forms of heating are bottled gas (butane or propane) and oil (kerosene or paraffin). Either of these is suitable provided the room is reasonably well ventilated and, again, provided the heater does not radiate too much light. Perhaps one of the best types of heater for the darkroom is the butane catalytic type. This is a very safe form of heating that has no flame. It relies on comparatively low-temperature chemical reactions to provide heat. It needs no flue but reasonable ventilation must be provided. The fumes, as with a properly maintained oil heater, are minimal and should give no trouble in the relatively short time you will normally spend in the darkroom. If you have any doubt about the adequacy of your ventilation, take a break every hour or so and open the door wide.

If you cannot manage to get the temperature up to 21°C and if you are happy to work in cooler surroundings, a waterbath will keep your developer up to the correct temperature. There are useful thermostatically-controlled immersible heaters supplied for aquaria and also sold by wine-making hobby shops and some photographic stores. One of these in a tray of water larger than your developing dish will keep your developer at the required temperature almost indefinitely. Such a heater can even be used quite satisfactorily for colour work with a processing drum if you divide the solutions up into small bottles and stand them in the tray along with the drum.

Basic Darkroom Equipment

How you equip your darkroom depends on the depth of your pocket and your attitude to the job in hand. The main objective is to make photographic prints. You can get by – and most people do – with the barest of essentials such as an enlarger, safelight, processing dishes, measuring flasks and storage bottles. You can also equip yourself with all the luxuries, such as exposure timers, meters, voltage and temperature control equipment, processing machines, print dryers and glazers, paper safes, colour analysers and so on. In this chapter, we deal with the more or less essential equipment. The accessories and other items that make life easier but do not necessarily improve the standard of work are left for the next chapter.

Enlarger construction

A photographic enlarger used to be a very simple instrument. All it needs is a source of light to illuminate a negative evenly and a lens to project the image of that negative on to a support for the paper on which the print is to be made. In its simplest form, the modern enlarger consists of a column mounted securely on a baseboard. An arm rides up and down the column and supports the enlarger head centrally over the baseboard. The head consists of a light-baffled lamphouse, containing the lamp and, below it, a piece of opal glass as a diffuser. The lamphouse sits on a negative carrier designed to hold the negative flat centrally under the lamp. Below that is the lens, mounted on a small bellows or a helical-thread tube for focusing.

That is all there is to the simplest of enlargers. A cable runs out of the top of the lamphouse for connection to the electricity supply and, when the lamp is switched on, the diffuser spreads the light reasonably evenly over the negative below it and, as the lens is moved up or down, the image of the negative is focused on the baseboard. Raising or lowering the head on the column allows the size of the projected image to be varied. The principle is exactly the same as that of the slide projector.

A more efficient arrangement is to replace the diffuser with a condenser lens, the function of which is to collect as much light as possible from the lamp and to concentrate it on to the negative area, thus providing brighter illumination and rather more contrast than the simple diffuser is capable of.

The focal length of the enlarger lens is generally similar to that of the standard lens on the camera–50 mm for 35 mm film, 75-80 mm for 6 × 6 cm and so on. The focal length of the lens controls the degree of enlargement possible at a given height of the head on the column. As in close-up photography, to which enlarging is also closely allied, a shorter focal length lens provides a larger image at a given separation between lens and image–but a shorter than standard lens needs careful design and manufacture to ensure even illumination and definition of the projected image. The few 'wide-angle' enlarger lenses available are consequently costly.

The focal length of the condenser lens is related to that of the projection lens. The condenser has to be of sufficient diameter to illuminate the negative evenly, commonly about 65 mm for 35 mm film and about 90 mm for 6 × 6 cm. It should have a focal length that allows an image of the lamp to be focused sharply within the projection lens. As the distance between lamp and projection lens varies, however, with the degree of enlargement, the position of the lamp should be variable too. There often is some provision for this but, as enlarger lamps are now commonly of the opal type, forming a relatively large, diffuse light source, critical focus of the lamp is not necessary.

The compromise focal length generally used for the condenser lens is about half that of the projection lens. It is possible to make such a lens for the 35 mm format from a single glass but for the larger formats such a lens would have to be extremely thick and it is general practice to make two separate lenses that, in combination, provide the focal length required. The lenses are generally of plano-convex construction (one flat side and one curving outward) and, when used in pairs, they are mounted in a metal housing with the convex sides inward.

Negative carriers

The straightforward negative carrier consists of two metal plates with central square or rectangular apertures of the negative size. The negative is sandwiched between these plates in such a way that the image area can be clamped squarely in the aperture. The carrier generally allows negatives to be inserted in strips and is placed into and removed from the enlarger via a slot between lamphouse and focusing unit.

The negative carrier for 35 mm film holds the film flat by pressure on the edges, exerted by the weight of the carrier itself, by pressure on the top plate from the head or by springs in the slot. For larger formats it is preferable that the negative be sandwiched between glass plates or, as the curl is toward the emulsion, at least held flat by a glass plate on top.

Negative carriers vary in design and sophistication. The basic elements are those described but they may consist simply of two separate plates or may be of complex construction, with a thin hinged top plate and a lower part housing a sliding red filter and shutters to vary the framing. In the more sophisticated enlargers, the carrier can be tilted to allow focus to be maintained during perspective corrections when printing from a negative with, for example, converging vertical lines. It may also be possible to turn the head on the column to project sideways to a wall or other support when the column height does not allow the degree of enlargement required. Alternatively, many enlargers allow the head to be swung round on the column to project over the back of the baseboard on to a lower surface or the floor, with suitable weighting of the baseboard.

However the enlarger is constructed, the basic requirements are that its supporting column be rigidly mounted on the baseboard and, if it is a vertical column, that it makes a perfect right angle with the baseboard. (There are some enlargers in which the supporting column slopes forward.) Whatever the type of column, the arm must support the head in such a way that the negative carrier is in a plane parallel with the baseboard and at right angles to the lens axis. The head must move freely on the column but it must, nevertheless, be possible to lock it positively at the exact height required. The lock may be mechanical, as is common with tubular steel columns, or it may be achieved by a friction drive mechanism, more common on square section columns. The friction-drive types must never be lubricated. They are often much slower in operation than, say, a tubular column with internal counterweight. They rely on the resistance to movement for maintaining a given setting.

Enlargers for colour work

The straightforward black-and-white enlarger contains little more of note but there are few enlargers now that do not take account of the fact that you might want to undertake colour printing. Unfortunately, the terminology applied to enlargers suitable for colour printing is not very precise.

One method of colour printing uses a set of just three—red, green and blue—filters held below the lens. It is called the additive system and calls for three separate exposures, one through each filter in turn. That, though perfectly practicable, is time-consuming and requires great care to ensure that no movement of the image occurs between exposures. The almost universal method of colour printing, however, uses magenta, cyan and yellow filters to subtract green, red and blue light respectively from the 'white' light of the enlarger lamp. This method is accordingly commonly known as the subtractive or white-light method.

The main requirement for colour printing is a set of filters to enable the colour of the light to be adjusted to suit various combinations of negative and paper. These filters are best placed between the lamp and the negative, where they have to be reasonably clean but do not have to be of optical quality, because they play no part in forming the image. If the top of the enlarger head is removable, it is easy enough, though not entirely satisfactory, to drop the required filters in on top of the condensers. From that, it was obviously only

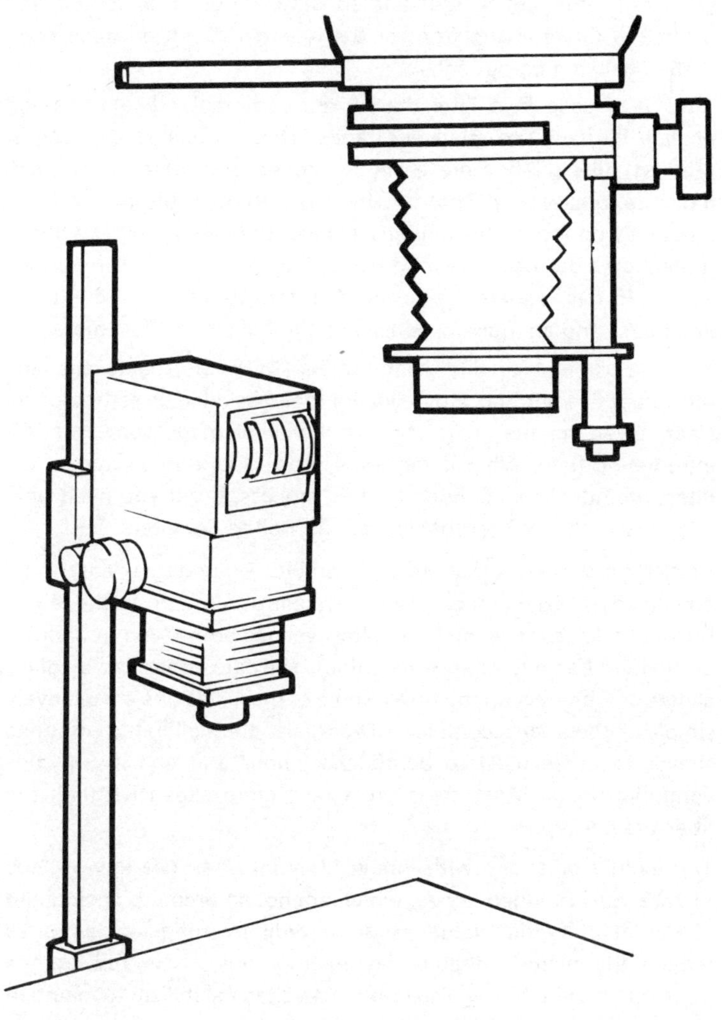

Colour printing needs provision for filters in the enlarger. A simple filter drawer above the negative holder may suffice or filtration may be built into the enlarger and operated by external controls.

a short step to modifying the ordinary enlarger in such a way that you could pull out a light-baffled drawer from that region and insert the filters at the front of the enlarger. Such an instrument is then called a colour enlarger.

The filters used in a filter drawer are commonly sheets of dyed acetate film and are relatively fragile. They are called CP (colour printing) filters. They are easily scratched and affected by heat, moisture, grease, etc. That is why it is not advisable to use them habitually on top of the condensers in an ordinary enlarger without protection from heat-resisting glass. They are supplied in various sizes (75 mm square being normal for 35 mm and 6 × 6 cm enlargers) and are quite expensive in the full set of 17 or more.

You can use high quality gelatin filters (CC filters) below the lens for subtractive printing. However, for that they must be scrupulously clean. Even so, they can degrade the print image somewhat by introducing flare. What is more the process is a little tedious. CP filters are not recommended for this process, but if you need only one or two, they will probably work as well as CC filters.

Rather than a set of filters in a drawer or under a lens, more advanced enlargers incorporate a system of filtration in the lamphouse. Fade-resistant dichroic filter wedges are moved in and out of the light beam to change its colour. They are controlled by dials, sliders or whatever on the front. Some of these designs are relatively simple, others are complex. The dials are calibrated in units similar to those used to define the colour and density of conventional filters. Most are a great deal more expensive than the filter-drawer type.

True colour enlargers with inbuilt filtration often use low-voltage (10-12 volt) halogen lamps, which are not so prone to ageing and alteration of colour value as is an ordinary tungsten lamp. To reduce the mains voltage, the enlarger has to be run from a transformer, which may also contain a voltage stabilizer to maintain constant colour and intensity from the lamp. Reflex illumination is also commonly used to protect negatives from the heat of the lamp. A filter drawer allows conventional filters to be used to augment the inbuilt arrangement. For black-and-white work the filter controls are turned to zero.

Additional features of enlargers

Enlarger manufacturers frequently offer convertible enlargers. The colour enlarger is the black-and-white version with the lamphouse changed. Everything above the condensers of the black-and-white enlarger can be easily removed and replaced by a colour head containing the colour filtration system. It is as well to bear this in mind when buying or replacing an enlarger. The black-and-white enlarger—provided it has a filter drawer—is perfectly satisfactory for colour printing, but the colour head makes life a lot easier. You simply dial infinitely variable filter values in, instead of constantly selecting rather fragile acetate filters and placing them in the filter drawer. If you intend to do a lot of colour printing, you may well find the high initial cost well worth while.

A feature of some enlargers that is not very common these days is an auto focus mechanism. As you raise or lower the head to alter the degree of enlargement, so the lens is automatically moved to maintain correct focus. The facility is generally limited to enlargements up to about 8 or 10x and is by no means essential. It is, however, very useful when you make a series of prints from parts of many negatives and therefore at different degrees of enlargement.

Some enlargers have rangefinders instead. You pull out a knob, or make some other adjustment, and the enlarger then projects a line image (instead of the negative) onto the baseboard. Adjusting the focus until this image is exactly continuous, focuses the enlarger. This is a useful but by no means essential feature.

A feature also becoming more commonly available is portability or, in some cases perhaps, transportability. There is one true portable 35 mm enlarger that packs away completely in a stout, small case like a small attaché case while many others can be dismantled and stowed away compactly in the original, reasonably durable packing. This can be a useful facility for those who have to clear the darkroom after each session.

Choosing an enlarger

Choosing your first enlarger is not an easy task. Sensible advice is to choose the most versatile type, ie, one that can handle more than one size of negative and that has a colour head available for subsequent upgrading. Ease of dismantling is never a bad feature, provided it does not affect rigidity and smooth, positive operation. In practice, an enlarger with all these features is rather expensive and there are cheaper versions that may suit your requirements perfectly until your financial situation improves. We have already detailed the essentials you should watch out for and there is very little to add. Fortunately, bad enlargers are rare, particularly among those offered by well-established manufacturers and, if your choice has to be governed totally by cost, you should still be able to produce quite satisfactory results.

Enlarger lenses

As important as the enlarger itself is the lens you fit to it. It is not more important because, no matter how good the lens, it cannot produce first class results unless the enlarger holds it, the negative and the lamphouse rigidly in position at all times. The lens is commonly an extra because there are relatively cheap lenses and very expensive ones. Again, the sensible advice is to go for the best you can afford–and again such advice can be modified.

Among the innumerable enlarger lenses on the market, there are a lot of comparatively inexpensive types that can give you all the quality you need when stopped down slightly and used for enlargements up to 8 or 10x. Indeed, in these conditions, even the most expensive lens could not better their performance–and they certainly exceed the capabilities of any camera lens used on an enlarger.

The construction principles for enlarger and camera lenses are entirely different. Theoretically at least, a lens gives its best performance at one object distance only. Certainly it is possible to design a lens that performs better at one fixed distance than the best of camera lenses–and at a fraction of the cost. An enlarging lens, is, in fact, designed to give optimum quality over a limited range of subject distances–the subject being the negative, which it is, in effect, photographing at close range. No ordinary camera lens is so constructed. It is designed to provide sharp images at subject distances from as far away as practicable to a metre or so from the

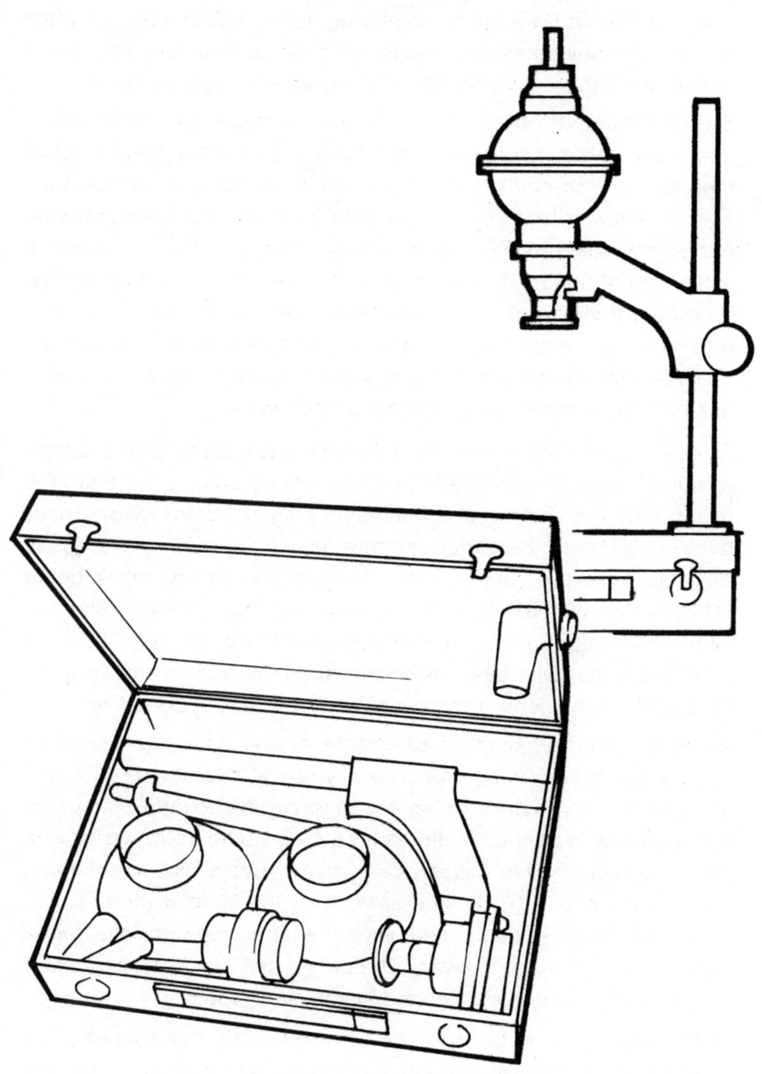

Portability is useful when space is limited. This enlarger packs away into a suitcase-like container that also serves as the baseboard.

lens. At closer range its performance is often noticeably poorer, as you may find in ultra close-up photography. In fact, you can often use a quite inexpensive enlarger lens on the camera and get a better result than with the camera lens at very close range.

So do not be put off by the fact that your resources are limited. A first-class enlarger lens (by reputation) can cost a great deal of money, but you can get excellent results for far less expenditure. The satisfaction that you can get from making your own prints far outweighs the possible disadvantage that you may run into a slight loss of quality if you push the lens beyond its true capability. If you are thinking of colour, you may paradoxically have less of a problem. Colour printing material is expensive and it is unlikely that you will often make prints of sufficient size to tax the capabilities of even a moderately-priced enlarger and lens.

Of course, enlarger lenses, like camera lenses, come with a variety of specifications. Most have apertures of between *f*2.8 and *f*5.6 for 50 mm and shorter, and between *f*4 and *f*5.6 for longer focus ones. In general, the wider aperture lenses are disproportionately more expensive. If your budget is limited, you will be much better off with a renowned *f*4 or *f*4.5 50 mm lens than with an unknown *f*2.8, for example. With a reasonably bright enlarger light, you can work quite happily, even in colour at *f*4 or *f*5.6. If you buy an *f*2.8 lens, choose one that has been reliably well reported on.

Another important point is to choose a lens with good aperture click stops. If you work with colour, you will need to select a lens aperture entirely in the dark, so you must be able to count the clicks easily. A few lenses offer illuminated stop numbers to assist with this. The exception to this advice is if you always use an enlarging meter, (see page 90). In that case, with the simpler models, you keep the time constant, and vary the aperture until the meter indicates the correct exposure. Of course, that can be at any point, not just at fixed intervals dictated by the click stops.

There can be one unexpected problem with the lowest-price lenses, though. The aperture may not close down evenly. That is a major difficulty. It means that you cannot safely assume that altering the time and changing aperture to compensate will give you the same print density.

Enlarging easel or masking frame

Ideas about essential accessories for an enlarger vary but it is difficult to manage without some form of masking frame. There are many designs but the basic function is the same. The masking frame (or enlarging easel) allows you to compose your pictures on the baseboard within the area of the paper size, fixes the position of the paper on the baseboard and holds it flat while you expose it. Additionally, it puts a white margin on the paper edges (or a black margin when you print from transparencies). In some cases, the margin is adjustable, while some types allow you to print out to the edges of the paper with no margin.

The orthodox or traditional masking frame consists of a flat metal base plate (usually metal because it needs to be reasonably heavy) with rubber or plastic feet to stop it sliding around on the baseboard. It has an L-shaped frame hinged to it at the top with a thin flexible metal strip attached to the top and left-hand side members by a clip that slides along a scale marked in centimetres and/or inches. The strips overlap so that as they are moved along the scale they enclose a rectangular area in the left hand top corner expanding outward to the maximum available on the baseplate. In use, the paper is held at the edges by the two fixed members and by the movable strips.

Masking frames that allow you to print without borders include one type with an adhesive-coated surface just tacky enough to grip the paper firmly but also to allow it to be easily removed. Another form uses L-shaped magnets with serrated inner edges to grip the paper. The magnets are available separately for use on any ferrous metal surface.

There are two essentials for a masking frame. First, it must provide square corners. That implies a reasonably robust construction of the fixed arms and a positive spring or friction grip of the sliding arms. Any slackness of the grip allows the attitude of the movable arms to vary and thus throw three corners out of square. Secondly, the scale marking must be clear and durable. You can generally use it in white light but it should be clear enough to be seen easily in safelighting. The finish of the surface is important, too. Scantily-painted metal is easily scratched and is then prone to rust. Whether the surface is black or white is a matter of personal preference. It is sometimes claimed that a white surface reflects the exposing light back into the print and so degrades it. Proof is hard to come by and even the theory is debatable.

A black surface requires you to place a sheet of white paper on it for composition and focus. Again, there is an incredibly hardy adage that says this is necessary in any case and that the paper should be the same thickness as the printing paper. What is the sense in focusing on one surface and then printing on another at a different distance?

Proof in this case is impossible as a simple depth of focus calculation shows. Enlarging is akin to close range photography. In effect, the enlarger lens is photographing the negative at extremely close range—true macro work in fact. In close-range photography, depth of focus (not depth of field) is relatively large. We need not go into details here but at, say 5x enlargement it is in the region of 3 mm at *f*4—regardless of lens focal length or negative size. At greater degrees of enlargement and, of course, at smaller apertures it is greater. So, if you print on anything more than 3 mm thick, you might think about using a substitute focusing surface—although, in fact, at 10x and *f*8, you would have a tolerance in paper position of about 11 mm, or nearly half an inch. This is depth of focus in either direction, but we are not really considering the possibility of the paper being lower than the masking frame.

Masking frames come in various maximum sizes from about 13 × 18 cm (5 × 7 inches) to 40 × 50 cm (16 × 20 inches). Buy the one that accommodates the largest size of print that you make frequently—not the largest you are ever likely to make. For most people that is either 20 × 25 cm (8 × 10 inches) or 20 × 25 cm (10 × 12 inches). Perhaps you will occasionally make larger prints but a large masking frame is a nuisance when you make small prints, whereas you can improvise for the occasional large print.

Exposure timer

When you expose the printing paper, you have to switch the enlarger lamp on, wait for the required time and then switch it off

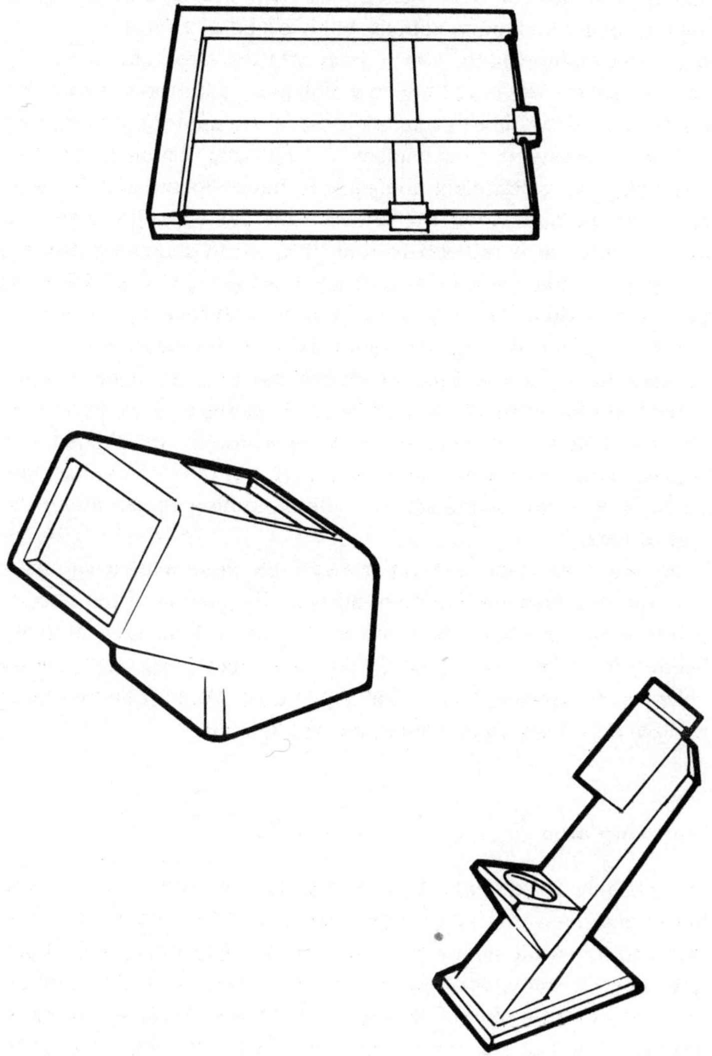

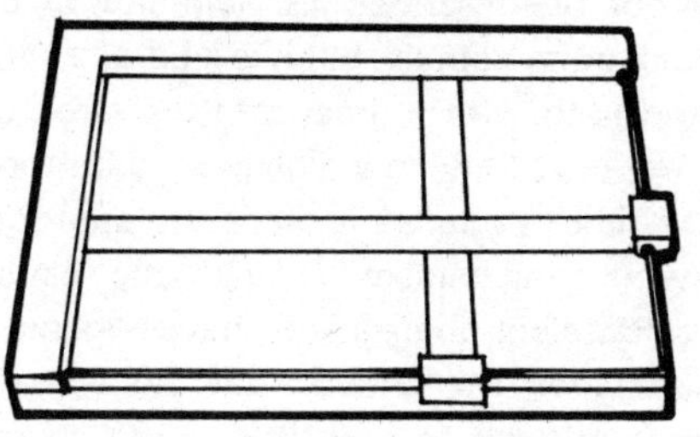

Darkroom aids. A masking frame is virtually essential to help you position the paper correctly, especially when colour printing.
Focusing magnifiers are not so vital but they can make focusing a lot easier, particularly with dense negatives.

again. That cannot be described as hard labour and plenty of people cope with it quite happily, but it is a bit of a chore.

A simpler method is to wire a timer into the lamp circuit so that you can set the required time on a dial, press a button to switch on the lamp and the timer switches it off at the appropriate time. An ordinary clockwork mechanism is perfectly satisfactory. Unfortunately, so-called electronic gadgets have become so universally accepted, perhaps even demanded, that the straightforward old clockwork timer is difficult to find. It is worth searching around, however, for the cheapest such instrument you can find. All it has to do is to switch the enlarger lamp on and off for set periods from about five seconds to 60 seconds maximum. It should also have a by-pass switch so that you can switch the lamp on independently of the timer for composition and focus. Anything else is elaboration. The timer does not even have to be accurate. Its alleged five seconds could be six or four or whatever, but that is not important provided it is always the same. There is nothing sacred about the unit of time.

There are more elaborate and considerably more expensive timers that perform the same function rather in the manner of the sledgehammer and the nut. There are those with 0.1 second intervals, believe it or not. Some of these instruments, especially those linked with exposure meters, have their uses, but they are not basic equipment, so we leave them to the next chapter.

Focusing aids

There is only one other enlarger accessory that might be considered basic, and even that is a border line case. It is certainly essential that you focus the image accurately on the baseboard and, if you have any difficulty, you might feel that a focus finder is essential. The function of a focus finder is to brighten and, usually, magnify a selected part of the baseboard image. There are two main types. Both intercept the image forming light rays with a mirror. The simplest then directs those rays an equivalent baseboard distance (just like the SLR camera) to a fine-ground screen. A highly polished mirror and a translucent screen make the image brighter and easier to focus. This type is small and easy to handle on almost any part of the image.

The second type has a much smaller mirror, with a separate focusing magnifier like a small telescope fixed at a convenient angle above it. A fine-line cross and semi-silvered mirror system allow you to focus the magnifier in the plane of the reflected image. You focus on the grain of the image, the blurb says, but not all of them have magnifiers that powerful. It is advisable to give this type of focus finder a trial before purchase if possible. Not everybody finds them easy to use—especially away from the centre of the image.

Developing tanks

Most of the rest of the equipment in the darkroom is concerned with processing prints and, to a lesser extent, films.

Taking films first, you need a developing tank. That is an absolute necessity for users of 35 mm or roll films (including the smaller cartridge-loaded films). No other form of processing is worth mentioning.

A developing tank is a cylindrical container with a push-on or screw-on lid that is lightproof but allows liquids to be poured in and out. Most types have a cap for the pouring vent so that the tank can be inverted to 'agitate' the developer. This disperses air-bells and prevents premature exhaustion of the solution closest to the film. The tank contains a spiral—a construction of grooves running to a central core so that a length of film (a 36-exposure length of 35 mm film is more than 150 cm or 5 feet in length) can be contained in a small space. The film is loaded into the spiral in total darkness, the spiral is placed in the tank body and the lid secured. All processing can then be carried out in room lighting or daylight.

Developing tanks and spirals are made from plastic or stainless steel. Some stainless steel versions have plastic lids. Each type has its advantages and disadvantages. Modern plastics are not easily shattered or distorted but the materials used in developing tanks may not withstand very hot solutions. Stainless steel bends relatively easily and a not-too-stoutly constructed spiral can distort beyond remedy if dropped. Naturally there are different qualities and good stainless steel types are virtually indestructible. Steel is a good thermal conductor (ie it conducts heat well). Plastics are quite good thermal insulators. During short developing times, solutions in a plastic tank will probably maintain their temperature accurately enough for black-and-white work even in relatively low ambient temperatures. In a metal tank, the solution temperature could drop a degree or two. On the other hand if you use a water bath to maintain solution temperatures, the metal tank should theoretically work better because it is a more efficient conductor. In practice it seems to make little difference, probably because the water bath serves more to keep the heat in than to transmit it from the outside.

Plastic spirals often have a self-load mechanism starting from the outer edge. You generally load a metal spiral from the central core outward. The plastic type can be easier to handle if it is kept scrupulously clean and dry. Nevertheless, each user swears by his own method and there is very little to choose between them in use or cost.

Tanks are supplied for a single 35 mm film or, in taller versions, to take several spirals, each with its own film. Rollfilm tanks can similarly take more than one film or the single film type may take two 35 mm spirals instead of the single 120 size. Most other sizes of film can be accommodated in special or adjustable spirals. There are types that can be loaded in daylight, those that take two films, back to back, in each spiral, and 120-size spirals that take 220-size film or two 120-size attached end to end.

The tanks can be used for processing both black-and-white and colour films, although some colour processing solutions—bleaches in particular—can attack metals. That is a thought worth bearing in mind; but all good stainless steel tanks are recommended—at least by their manufacturers—for colour processing.

Thermometers and stirring rods

An absolute necessity for processing films is a thermometer. It would be nice to say that the only reliable thermometer is a certified

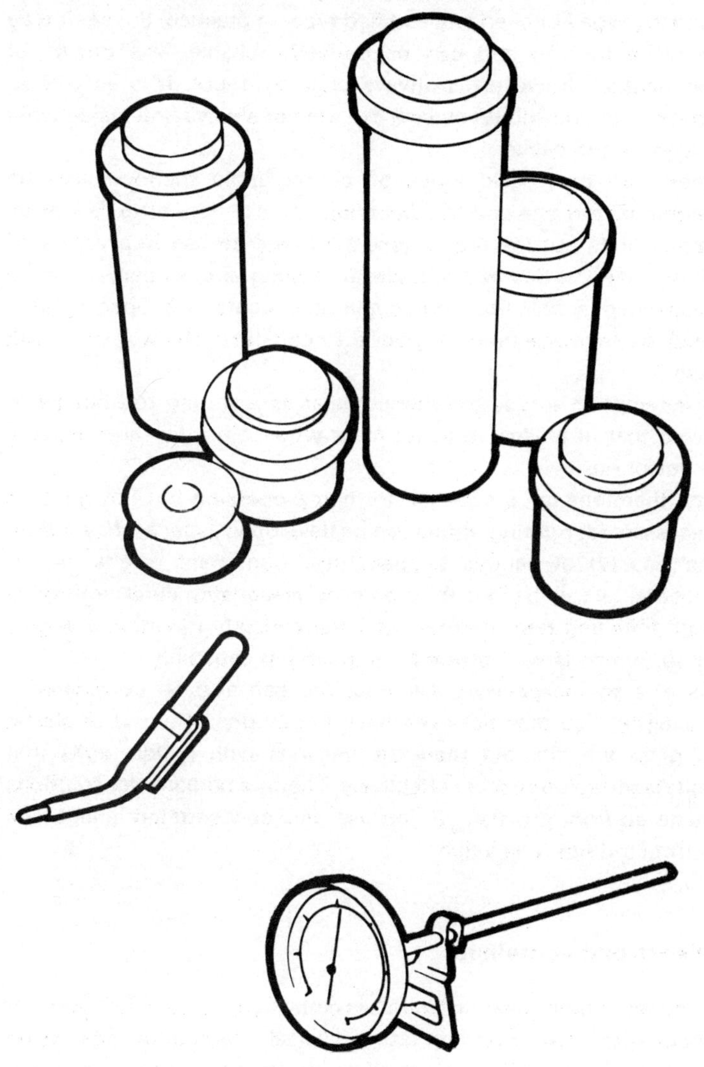

Developing tanks come in a variety of sizes to take 35 mm or 120 size film and can often be adapted to take other sizes. The film is wound on to a reel that is then inserted into the tank body. Multi-reel types are available. Thermometers are supplied in various types, including those with dials and a 'bent' version for use in a dish.

mercury type–or even any certified type. In practice, the spirit type is easier to read and can be perfectly reliable. The quality of certification, however, is always open to doubt. It is as well to check it for yourself if you can. You do not always find inside what it says on the packet.

There are two basic types of photographic thermometer–the traditional rod one and the dial type. The dial may have its special applications but the rod is generally easier to use in a variety of circumstances. Secured in a plastic, sprung clothes peg, it can be suspended in dish, flask, bottle and other containers. Special 'bent' versions are made for dishes but they can get in the way in a small dish.

It is tempting to use the thermometer as a stirring rod but try to avoid that. It makes an awful mess when it breaks–and mercury is poisonous.

The thermometer is essential for film processing but not quite so necessary for printing. Prints can be developed as far as they will go (to finality) at various temperatures. Consistent results in film processing can be obtained only by reasonably strict control of both time and temperature–the latter certainly to within a degree or so, which is well beyond any guessing capability.

As it is so inexpensive, a stirring rod can also be considered a necessity. You may not even have to buy one. Any rod of plastic or glass will do, but there are versions with paddle ends that agitate the solution more effectively. They are primarily for solutions made up from powders. If you use only concentrated liquids, the stirring rod has little value.

Dishes and containers

If money is hard to come by, this is certainly an area where you can economize. The more or less universal method of processing black-and-white prints in a small darkroom is to use three relatively shallow dishes–for developer, water rinse or stop bath, and fixer. The genuine photographic variety of dish is not terribly expensive but it can cost significantly more than similar trays sold by garden supply stockists as gravel trays.

A photographic developing dish generally has a pouring lip and raised strips on the bottom to make removal of the print easier. It may even have a groove to hold a thermometer. A gravel tray can be virtually identical but without the pouring lip or the thermometer groove. It is frequently more substantial than some of the light-weight developing trays that always seem to be in danger of folding up under the weight of the solution. Photographic dishes are generally white, although different-coloured types are sometimes sold in sets to allow you to keep one for fixer and one for developer. Gravel trays tend to be green, brown or grey. The only real snag is that gravel trays are not made to photographic paper sizes and you might have to hunt around to find a suitable shape.

As with a masking frame, buy dishes of a size for comfortable working with your usual size of print. The bigger the dish the more solution it needs and that can be unnecessarily expensive. If you habitually make both large and small prints, you might consider two sets of dishes.

The solutions that go in the dishes have to be stored. Here, too, there are special photographic products and there are beer bottles. It is wise to avoid containers that might allow their contents to be mistaken for beverages but that depends entirely on the conditions of use. Never put a photographic solution into a bottle with a drink label still on it. If you have a temporary darkroom, and there is any chance of bottles getting mixed up, do not use drinks bottles at all.

The variety of containers available is so wide that no specific recommendations can be made. You may be a large user and store your developer and fixer in 20-litre plastic 'jerricans'. You may use concentrated solutions and need nothing larger than a one-litre bottle.

The advantage of containers produced for photographic use is that they are frequently made from durable materials and have efficient stoppers. They can therefore be squeezed to expel air and thus prevent developer from oxidizing. There are special squeeze bottles with extra wide necks for easy pouring. These squash down concertina fashion to reduce the volume of air remaining as solutions are used.

Measuring vessels

To obtain the correct volume of solution for your developing tank or to make up solutions, you need measures. These are in the form of beakers or flasks with scales marked down the side. You can use domestic types but their markings are more likely to be suspect than on those designed for photography. That is a generalization, of course, and you must be wary of the photographic type, too.

Most measuring flasks are plastic and some plastics discolour badly with age. As they discolour the markings become less legible. Buy the clear type if possible but make sure that the scale is not simply printed on. It will inevitably wear off in time. You need two or three sizes according to your working methods. If you regularly measure 50 ml or less, get one measure with no greater capacity than 100 ml. Measuring small quantities in a large beaker can lead to considerable inaccuracy. The 500 ml and one-litre sizes are all that you are likely to need in the larger sizes but you may like to double up on a particular size so that you can keep one for fixer and one for developer. With the better quality materials that is not really necessary provided you wash them thoroughly after use.

If you are at all doubtful about your ability to clean your measuring vessel between solutions, make up your chemicals in the order that you will use them. Naturally, all processes can stand some forward contamination. Few can stand even the merest trace of backward contamination without losing some picture quality.

Miscellaneous accessories

There are many small items that are useful but not vital in the average darkroom. If you are worried about your sartorial appearance, for example, or are just dead clumsy, a laboratory apron is a good investment. Water and chemical resistant, it might just avert a disaster. Colour processing bleach has an interesting effect on fabrics.

Film clips simplify the hanging up of films to dry. They grip the film securely and have hooks or holes for hanging on line or nail, etc. They are sufficiently weighty to stop the film curling up on itself.

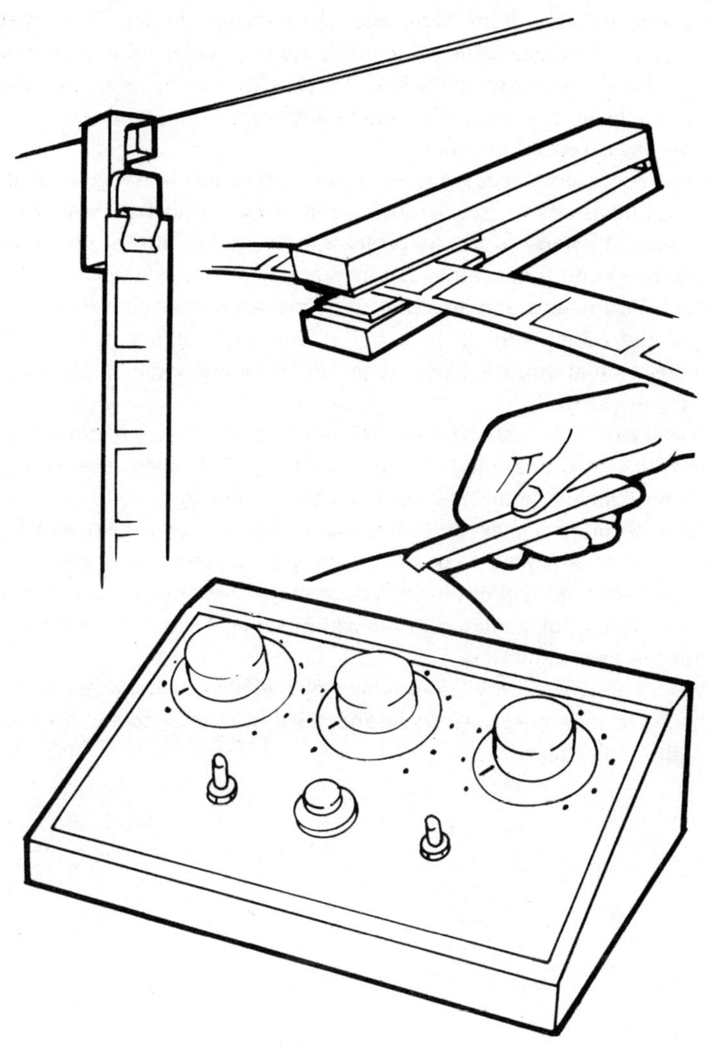

More darkroom aids. Film clips allow you to suspend the film safely for drying. Excess moisture can be first wiped off with special squeegee tongs. Ordinary print tongs make paper handling less messy. An exposure timer switches the enlarger lamp off automatically.

Film wipers in the form of chamois or foam covered tongs remove excess moisture from films and allow faster drying. They may prevent drying marks, too, but if they are not treated with care, they can also put marks on to the film. A more elaborate type, known as a print squeegee, is specially designed for removing excess moisture from resin-coated papers.

Print tongs are a necessity for black-and-white printing. It really is not advisable to paddle about in developer and fixer with your fingers. Perhaps a lot of professionals do it; but professional practice is not necessarily synonymous with good practice in any field. You need two pairs, one to be contaminated with fixer only and the other with developer. Get different colours or different types so that you never mix them up. They are made in plastic or stainless steel.

If you habitually use that type of cassette that needs a hammer and vice to remove its end, there is a device for 'effortless opening of 35 mm film cassettes' that does not break the bank.

Look through a mail order catalogue. They have almost endless lists of small items that will make you wonder how you ever managed to do without them. You may go further and wonder why you should not continue to do without them. After all, you never felt the need until now.

We have avoided full descriptions of paper and chemicals so far because they are really basic and need a chapter to themselves. That comes later.

Darkroom Accessories

We have dealt with the basic necessities for the average small darkroom. There are many more items of equipment that are extremely useful but far from essential. Some of them, indeed, could be called rather unnecessary luxuries. On the other hand, once you start getting involved in colour, anything that cuts down the tedium of some of the work involved is welcome.

Exposure timers

We indicated in the previous chapter that a simple clockwork timer was perfectly satisfactory. That is true, but most people are now accustomed to electronic or electrical gadgetry that is sometimes easier to use and often looks more elegant. The exposure timer is a good case in point.

Unfortunately, many manufacturers seem to have gone in for overkill, competing with each other to produce the most sophisticated timer possible. The main requirements for a good, efficient timer for black-and-white work and, indeed, most colour work, is that it should provide timed lamp switching from about five seconds to 60 seconds. Shorter exposures are unnecessary; longer exposures are rarely required and are not critical to a few seconds. For colour work, long exposures can lead to disastrous reciprocity failure effects. In any case, it is not difficult to press the timer button twice or more.

The timer should have a by-pass switch for composition and focus and the ability to repeat a set exposure indefinitely. Anything beyond that is totally unnecessary for an instrument designed only to time the exposure. A very few inexpensive timers confine themselves to this modest specification. Most go far beyond it with refinements that you have to pay for but rarely use, such as the ability to measure 1/10 second intervals. They all claim superb accuracy, but how often do you refer to previous records for the exposure time you gave to a previous print on a different timer? That is the only time when accuracy is important.

Exposure meters

The accuracy of a timer may be important if you use it in conjunction with a separate exposure meter. The meter tells you what exposure you want and you set the timer accordingly. Most such instruments are, however, calibrated together from test strips. They may even be incorporated in the same instrument.

An enlarger meter may read the light reflected from the enlarger baseboard or it may be placed in the light beam to read either an integrated density or a particular tone. The principle is simple enough and there are a few such meters available for black-and-white work that are not too expensive. Others go a little further and assess the contrast of the image and recommend a suitable paper grade. Yet others are usable for both black-and-white and colour. The simpler meters are not programmed with the exposure time. You keep that constant, and adjust the lens aperture to give the correct light level.

In use, you first produce as perfect a print as possible by test strip or trial and error methods and note the exposure required. You then have to calibrate the meter to give the same exposure for the same conditions. The calibration varies according to design but rarely involves more than turning a knob and noting its setting. You then use the same setting for further prints on that batch of paper processed in the same chemicals for the same length of time and at the same temperature. For convenience, note the setting on the paper box—or in your darkroom notebook.

Automatic exposure

We have had automatic-exposure cameras for a long time, so there should be nothing strange in the concept of an automatic-exposure enlarger. In theory at least, the technique should be easier. Few automatic cameras measure the illumination in the focal plane, but many enlarger meters do. Automatic devices have a sensor suspended above the baseboard, (out of the beam from the lens) reading a relatively large area, typically 10 × 15 cm or more. There is no great difficulty in transmitting the reading to a timer controlling a switch in the enlarger lamp supply.

Such instruments are available with various degrees of sophistication and at correspondingly varying prices. Among the lowest in price but typical of the genre is a model consisting of a neat box measuring about 15 × 9 × 6 cm (6 × $3\frac{1}{2}$ × $2\frac{1}{2}$ inches) connected to a sensor on a stand about 13 cm high with a large flat foot that allows it to stand at the edge of the masking frame. A coiled lead connects the unit to the electricity supply while the enlarger lamp lead (or transformer lead for a low voltage lamp) is plugged into a socket on the case. There are switches for on/off, function and expose. The three position function switch sets the instrument for automatic working, bypass for composition and focus, and manual to allow the push button expose switch to be used manually. A calibration dial has settings from one to 11 for various paper and process conditions.

To use the meter you make test prints or strips with the dial set arbitrarily to a near-central position to start and to higher or lower positions as the tests indicate. When you have the best possible print, note the setting and use it subsequently for prints on that batch of paper with the same chemistry–regardless of lens, aperture, magnification, type of negative or whatever. To work automatically after calibration, you set the function switch to the auto position and press the expose switch. The enlarger lamp switches on and off automatically and repeats the operation each time the expose switch is pressed.

Naturally, such a system eliminates the need for a separate timer. The most basic model does not, in fact, give any indication of the exposure duration. Other models incorporate a digital readout of the exposure time.

One very important point must be borne in mind when using any type of enlarging meter–and especially the type that reads off the baseboard. The sensor measures all illumination it picks up, including that from the safelight. The paper is not sensitive to safelight illumination but the sensor is and correspondingly gives shorter exposure when the safelight is on than when it is off. That is taken care of by your original calibration provided you do not change the lens aperture or the degree of enlargement. Once you do that the relationship between image illumination and safelight illumination varies. The result is that a metered exposure of ten seconds at *f*4 may become only 15 seconds or so at *f*5.6 or about 25 at *f*8, giving underexposed prints. So either switch off the safelight when using a meter or shield the baseboard from its direct light.

This type of meter is fully automatic. Others are semi-automatic in that the exposure is determined by adjusting timing knobs before the expose button is pressed. Either type can be of considerable help in printing but, like most automatons, they have their limitations.

For straight prints from good negatives, they can be perfect. If you are straining for the best possible print, they produce your 'starter' efficiently but have to be disconnected or switched to manual for any selective exposure work.

Colour analysers

Most enlarging exposure meters can be used with black-and-white or colour materials but exposure is not the aspect of colour work that gives the most trouble. The composition of the filter pack is the problem that has caused many beginners to give up prematurely. When you have built up a store of experience in colour printing, you wonder what all the fuss was about, because you learn to assess an off-colour print accurately and to correct it by changing the filtration. When you start, this seems to be an insurmountable problem. No matter what you do, success comes slowly, and the pile of discarded pieces of very expensive colour paper grows alarmingly.

Electronics can solve this problem, too, by means of another instrument known as a colour analyser. These vary tremendously in price but there are relatively inexpensive models (in terms of good camera or enlarger prices) that are perfectly adequate for the so-called amateur market. Manufacturers have learned over the years, of course, that the term 'professional' or even a high price tag is an irresistable lure for many hobby photographers with more money

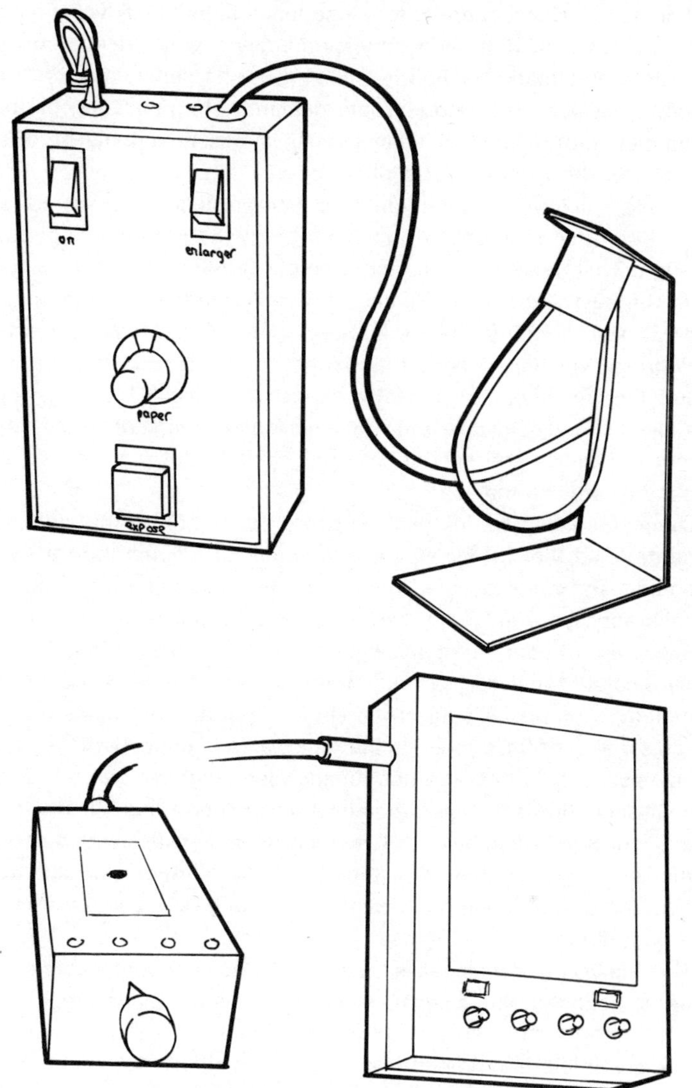

Automatic exposure control can be fitted to enlargers by various means. This instrument is described in the text. The colour analyser *(bottom)* is a simple version with LED indicators. Advanced versions have calibrated setting knobs and a meter dial in place of the LEDs.

than sense. Consequently, they frequently aim their advertising of highly-sophisticated (and correspondingly highly-priced) equipment at this market, when its specification is generally such that only a research laboratory would demand. The practising photographer, professional or amateur, can almost invariably produce equal results with far less sophistication.

To use a colour analyser, you must first produce a perfect colour print by other methods—a statement that will raise many a hollow laugh. That, however, is a fact of colour printing life, so you must do the best you can. There are a few tips in a later chapter and a great deal more information in Jack Coote's *Focalguide to Colour Printing.* You must make this perfect, or reference, print from a suitable negative, ie, perfectly exposed, typical of the type of subject you usually take and with a reasonable range of colours and tones. Sunsets and silhouettes are definitely out, unless all your pictures are like that.

Once you have your 'perfect' exposure, you set the colour analyser controls so that it indicates a zero centre or null setting for each colour, and for exposure. This is in effect the same operation as calibrating your enlarging exposure meter; but it takes account of the colour of your filter pack and negative as well as light intensity. The colour analyser settings form a 'programme' suitable for negatives of similar subjects in similar lighting conditions on the same make of film, printed on the same batch of paper with the same chemistry. To print another, unanalysed negative, you set the analyser controls to the programme figures, then adjust the filtration and lens aperture to balance the image characteristics with those of the reference negative. You then have the filtration and aperture required to produce a print from the new negative, using the same exposure time.

The analyser generally takes the form of a box of complicated electronic gadgetry with a separate probe containing a photomultiplier or other powerful sensor with movable filters that set it to read one primary colour at a time. It has a meter or a simple system of light-emitting diodes (LEDs) that you have to bring to a null position by adjusting programme control knobs when analysing the reference negative, then to the same position by altering filtration and lens aperture when balancing another negative.

It is a remarkably simple procedure but a fresh programme has to be set for each type of subject, as well as for different makes and batches of paper and film, and different chemistry. That is not as difficult as it sounds but it does mean building up quite a library of reference negatives if your subjects are varied.

There are a few short cuts, such as using a grey card included in the subject area of each negative or in the first of a batch. You use that as your reference tone for analysis instead of the flesh tone, green grass, etc. of various separate subjects. Some workers like to use the film rebate as their reference tone. The point is that whatever you use as your reference colour, the instrument tries to reproduce any other tone that it analyses as that colour. If, therefore, you use a flesh tone in a portrait as your original reference and then switch to a grey card area for the next negative, the analyser will try to give the filtration and aperture to reproduce the grey card area as a flesh tone.

As an alternative to reading from a specific tone, you can diffuse the image to form a homogeneous colour and density. This 'integrated' recording is the same as you get with a normal camera exposure meter. It is also the way that commercial colour printers measure colours for printing. It works well for most pictures. It does not work for any unusual subject, such as a close up of a face, or a close up of a coloured door.

Processing drums

The traditional three dishes for processing prints can be replaced by processing drums or machinery. Processing drums appeared some years ago to make colour printing easier for the occasional or small-quantity user. They resemble multiple developing tanks, consisting essentially of a plastic tube (some colour solutions attack metal) with a light-tight cap through which liquids can be poured. The idea is that you put a sheet of exposed colour paper in the tube in darkness and secure the lid. You can then turn on the light. To process the print, you successively pour in and out the various processing solutions (in quite small quantities—as little as 50 ml), agitating the drum continuously and the job is done. There are now many different brands of chemistry for such processors, using only two or three solutions.

Processing drums are also recommended for black-and-white work for perfectionists who believe in the once-only use of all chemicals. Used thus, they should certainly provide absolute consistency—vital for colour printing, but not quite so essential in black-and-white. Their greatest disadvantages are the need for continual agitation and the limited capacity, often just one 20 × 25 cm print or two smaller ones at a time. After each use they have to be thoroughly washed and dried, which can be a bit of a chore in a darkroom without running water.

A mechanical device can replace continuous hand agitation. These come in various forms, some imparting a two-way action that both turns and tips the drum to provide an end to end as well as a circular movement of the solution. Temperature control can also be built in with space for bottles of water in a water jacket. All these elaborations are a boon to the colour printer; but you can produce perfectly good prints without them.

Stabilization printing

A type of printing that suffered a set-back with the advent of faster-processing resin-coated papers was until then becoming popular and is still widely used. Generally known as stabilization processing, it uses paper with a developing agent, usually hydroquinone, incorporated in the emulsion. This enables it to develop fully in a few seonds when merely dampened with an activator solution (usually based on caustic soda).

The method is to expose the paper in the normal way by contact or projection and to feed it between rollers that pick up activator from a dish. From these rollers it passes under guides that dunk it in a stabilizer solution and thence to other rollers that squeegee it damp dry. It emerges from the other end of the machine as a fully processed print that will retain its image for many months. It will eventually fade because the stabilizer is not a permanent fixer. The print can, however, be fixed in the normal solutions at any subsequent time.

Stabilization processors are made in various forms—and can even

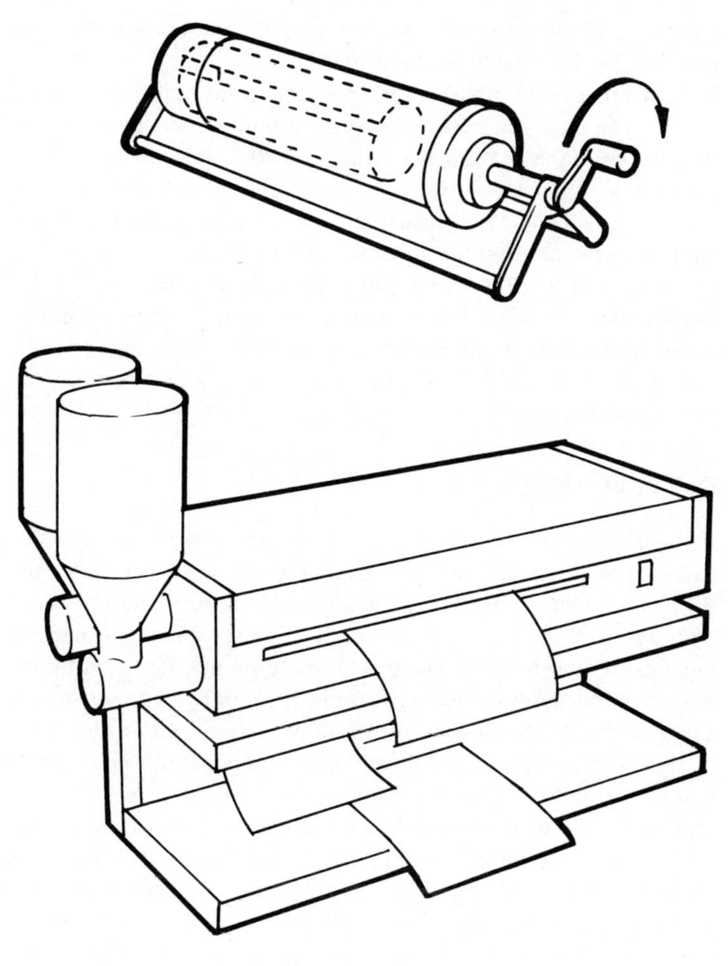

Many designs of colour processing drum are available. This type provides rotary and end-to-end movement to avoid streaky processing.
Stabilization printing machines *(bottom)* are for the rapid production of black-and-white prints.

be improvised from some of the old wet-process copying machines, which worked in virtually the same way but often with only two sets of rollers. The current machines may have six or more sets of rollers and a feed system that keeps the solution trays topped up and empties them rapidly for replenishment.

The advantages of stabilization processing are speed and space saving. The time you need to produce a print depends on its size. It moves smoothly through the machine, a 20 × 25 cm print passing through in 45 seconds or less. The width of material taken is commonly 35 cm (14 inches) or 50 cm (20 inches) and the length is unlimited, yet the larger machine occupies no more bench space than 91 × 25 × 14 cm (36 × 10 × 5½ inches).

Stabilization paper is much more expensive than ordinary bromide paper (the standard product) and a little more expensive than the resin-coated papers designed for rapid processing in more-or-less orthodox solutions.

Colour processors

Processing drums are limited in their print handling capacity. Because the chemicals can be toxic, and safelighting virtually nil, dish processing is not recommended for colour materials. So, if you want to process a dozen or so prints together, especially large ones, you have to spend a lot more money for a full-blown machine. Processing machinery of this type, once designed almost exclusively for commercial use, is now coming within the reach of smaller darkroom operators and even the non-professional who takes a lot of colour pictures.

One type follows broadly the same principle as stabilization processors but is essentially a little more complicated. It has to have temperature control because many colour processes work at a relatively high temperature and are much less tolerant of variations than black-and-white processes. As the process time is virtually unalterable in most machines, it must be possible to vary the temperature so that the machine can handle more than one process. The amount of solution fed into the machine is generally much greater, one model taking, for example 2.5 litres each of developer and bleach-fix. A stop bath is interposed in this model to counteract the travelling time through the rollers (9 cm a minute) between the two essential baths. Finally, the width of material the machine can handle is less than that of most stabilization processors at about 20 cm (8 inches). This particular machine measures 84 × 42 × 21 cm (about 33 × 16 × 8 inches) and weighs 16 kg (35 lb). Above all, it is expensive, costing quite a bit more than most colour enlargers.

Less expensive but still at around the price of an average colour enlarger is a tank-type processing box designed primarily for Ektacolor prints. The paper is suspended in the solutions in double-sided paper holders giving a total capacity of twelve 20 × 25 cm prints or a corresponding number of smaller prints. The machine can process to completion in four minutes at 37°C (100°F). It occupies only about 37 × 27 cm ($14\frac{1}{2} \times 10\frac{1}{2}$ inches) of bench space.

Yet another approach is supplied by the laminar-flow type of machine that has a capacity of one 28 × 36 cm (11 × 14 inch) sheet at a time (or a corresponding number of smaller sheets) and has to be hand-fed. Nevertheless it is much easier to operate than a processing drum. It is a flat-bed machine in which the solutions flow evenly over a platen on which the exposed print is laid. The solutions pass between the print surface and the platen and do not wash over the back of the print.

The solutions have to be poured into a trough by hand but are pumped out again. Wash water between solutions is also pumped through from an inbuilt tank or can be poured into the trough.

There are models with and without temperature control. The control is not essential, but does make life easier. The machine incorporates a tempering trough to hold 300 ml (11 oz) containers (supplied) and to hold their contents at the correct temperature. It is the contents of these containers that are poured into the machine for each print and circulated by the pump. It is therefore evident that any process can be handled–black-and-white or colour, paper or film–no matter how many solutions are required. All operations are in full lighting after establishing the developer flow and positioning the print.

This is the least expensive of the machines we have described and is claimed to be the most economical of any process including drums. It does not dump the chemicals after use. They are pumped out into the original containers and can be replenished for subsequent use. The machine measures 56 × 40 × 28 cm (22 × 16 × 11 inches) and weighs about 4.5 kg (10 lb) empty. Its tank capacity is about 13.5 litres (3 gallons) and the filled weight is about 18.5 kg (41 lb). A larger model, to take material up to 40 × 58 cm (16 × 23 inches) is also available at about twice the price.

Paper storage

If you find it tedious to store photographic paper in its original packing and to extract each sheet as required, you can buy a paper safe. These are enclosed trays or drawers with light-trapped slots through which paper is pushed as you turn a knob or similar control. They are rather expensive for the simplicity of their construction and have the disadvantage that you can store only one size and type of paper in each safe. If you use various combinations of sizes, grades, etc., you need a safe for each.

You may find it more satisfactory to construct a light-tight drawer under your bench or enlarger baseboard. Then you can fit dividers to separate the various sizes, etc, that you commonly use and, perhaps, provide labelled covers for both identification and additional protection. Yet more protection can be provided by wiring in a switch that breaks the circuit between the white light and the electrical supply. The light then goes out when the drawer is opened and cannot be switched on again until the drawer is shut. There is no protection against other light entering the darkroom, so you must make sure that drawer is truly light-tight and is shut before you leave the darkroom.

Making proof prints

It is a waste of printing paper to make enlargements from every negative just because you cannot see the reversed image clearly. Contact prints, even from 35 mm negatives, can generally show you whether a larger print is worth the time and expense.

Various types of proof printer are available, the most popular being the type that allows you to print the complete roll of film in one operation on a 20 × 25 cm (8 × 10 inch) sheet of paper–35 mm film cut into strips of six and 120 film into strips of four. Basically, this type of printer is simply a baseboard to hold the paper, hinged to a clear plastic plate with holders for the negative strips. Negatives and paper are held in close contact, emulsion to emulsion, and illuminated by the enlarger beam or other source for a compromise exposure for the whole film.

It is hardly less convenient in practice to place a suitable sheet of bromide paper on the enlarger baseboard with the head at a sufficient height to enable the beam through the lens to illuminate it evenly. On the paper (emulsion up) you can then lay the negative strips (emulsion down) and press them together with a sheet of plate glass. Switch on the enlarger (with no negative in the carrier) for the required exposure time and then develop the paper in the normal way.

Drying and glazing prints

Now that resin-coated paper is so commonly used, print glazing is becoming less popular. It was always a difficult process with amateur type equipment and many people avoided using glossy paper for that purpose. A good glaze, however, undoubtedly improves the appearance of a glossy-paper print and such a surface is necessary for the best delineation of very fine detail.

A print is glazed by bringing it into contact with a highly polished surface while the emulsion is wet and relatively soft and allowing it to dry there. When it peels off, the high gloss of the glazing surface is reproduced on the print–together with any previously invisible spots of dust or other blemishes that were on the glazing surface. The difficulty with the relatively small flat-bed glazers supplied to the amateur market is in establishing and maintaining perfect contact between the glazing plate (stainless steel, chromed brass, etc.) and in excluding dust. The plates have to be treated with extreme care and washed carefully after each use.

The machines consist essentially of a box enclosing a heating element. Attached to the back edge is a framework for a cloth blanket or apron that clamps over the front edge to tension the apron and hold the print down. The box generally has a curved surface to assist in this operation. The wet print is pressed into contact with a separate glazing plate that is then placed on the box with the print upward. The heater is switched on and the apron clamped in position. When the print is dry the blanket is lifted and the print drops off the plate with a perfect glaze—if you are lucky. The machine can be used without the glazing plate as a dryer only or without the heat as a cold glazer. The only advantage of using heat for glazing is that it is quicker. There is no difference in the glaze. The machines are supplied in a variety of sizes that are not very closely related to paper sizes. A dryer/glazer is not a very expensive item, nor is it very necessary for most people.

If you use resin-coated paper exclusively, you have no use for a dryer/glazer at all, because these papers must not be subjected to excessive heat. There are thermostatically-controlled models that you might risk using at the recommended temperature, but it *is* a risk. There are special dryers for RC papers but they are unbelievably expensive for the job they do. These materials dry very quickly indeed at room temperature, especially if they are wiped with a clean chamois leather to remove excess moisture or blotted with photographic blotting paper.

If that is not quick enough, you can speed up the process with a hair dryer—but you may overheat the print, or blow dust onto it.

Drying films

If you want to make prints from your films as soon as possible after the film comes out of the tank, you need a drying cabinet or some similar arrangement. Films can take an hour or two to dry naturally, and, until they are dry, the emulsion is very susceptible to damage; and to dust which sticks to it.

The usual drying method is to attach film clips to top and bottom and hang the strip of film somewhere where the cat cannot get at it. It should be in as draught-free a place as possible so that no house dust or debris can be blown on to the tacky emulsion before it is completely dry. Similarly it is unwise to attempt to accelerate the process with a hair dryer or fan heater. Some of these can ruin

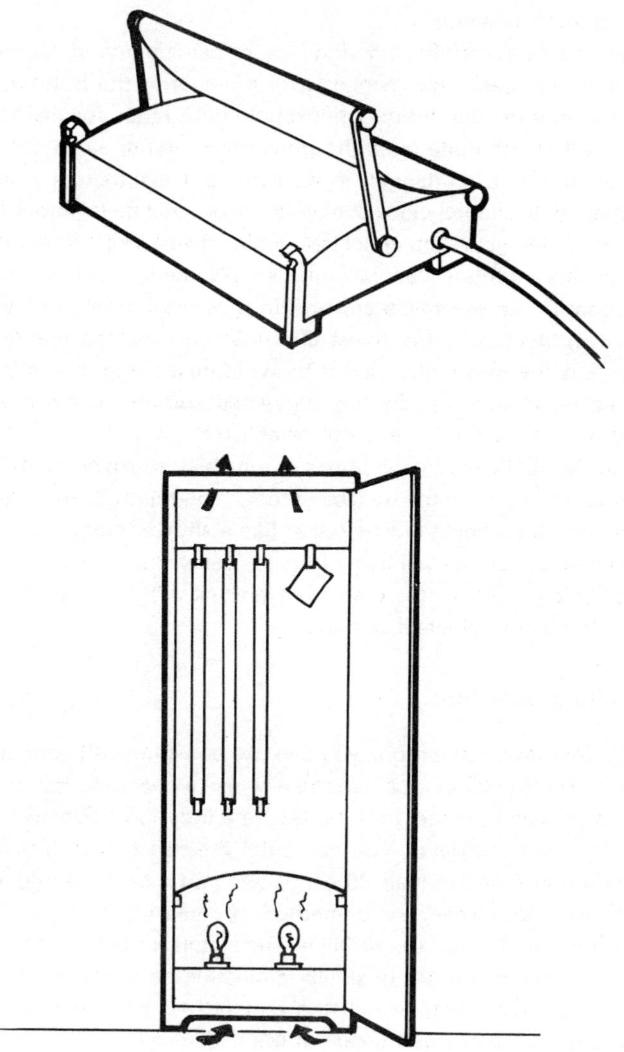

A dryer/glazer speeds up the drying process and, when used with a glazing sheet, puts a hard glaze on glossy papers.
Film drying can be accelerated in a drying cabinet. The metal shield over the lamps should leave space at the sides to allow warm air to rise past it.

a film in five seconds flat as they propel tiny dust particles like bullets into the emulsion.

If you must have artificial drying, buy or make a drying cabinet—a tall thin cupboard arrangement with a heater at the bottom. You can use one or two ordinary household light bulbs for the heater. They will create quite enough updraught of warm air to dry films rapidly and with no danger of overheating. Nevertheless, position a curved or V-shaped piece of aluminium or other metal above them to protect the films from direct heat and to divert drops from the hot bulbs. The structure can be quite simply made from wood and hardboard. The essentials are openings at the bottom, below the heater, protected by the finest filter material you can improvise—muslin, nylon mesh, etc. That is to avoid dust being drawn in and carried up to the films by the convected current. At the top you need outlets for the warm air to establish the current from bottom to top. Naturally, you need hooks or whatever to suspend the films from and the door must be close fitting. You might even make the outer skin from sheet plastic rather like a shower curtain provided you keep the lamps well away from it. Make sure the wiring to the lamp bulbs is well protected from any possible water splashes. Earth the lamp holders if possible.

Handling bulk film

Once you have a darkroom, you can use bulk film with confidence. If you have to black out a cupboard or use a changing bag to load cassettes, you may feel that the task is a little too troublesome. In the darkroom, however, you can cut 1.5 m or so from a 5, 17 or 30 m roll of film and load 36 exposures into a cassette with ease. You have to devise some method of measuring the required length but that is not too difficult. The simplest method is to hook a perforation over a nail or similar projection on the bench or door jamb and then carefully pull the required length out to another mark that you can easily locate in the dark.

That is a bit fiddly, however, and you would be better advised to get hold of a bulk film loader. Then, of course, you do not need the darkroom, because only loading the roll of film into its chamber needs to be done in darkness. There are several models of bulk

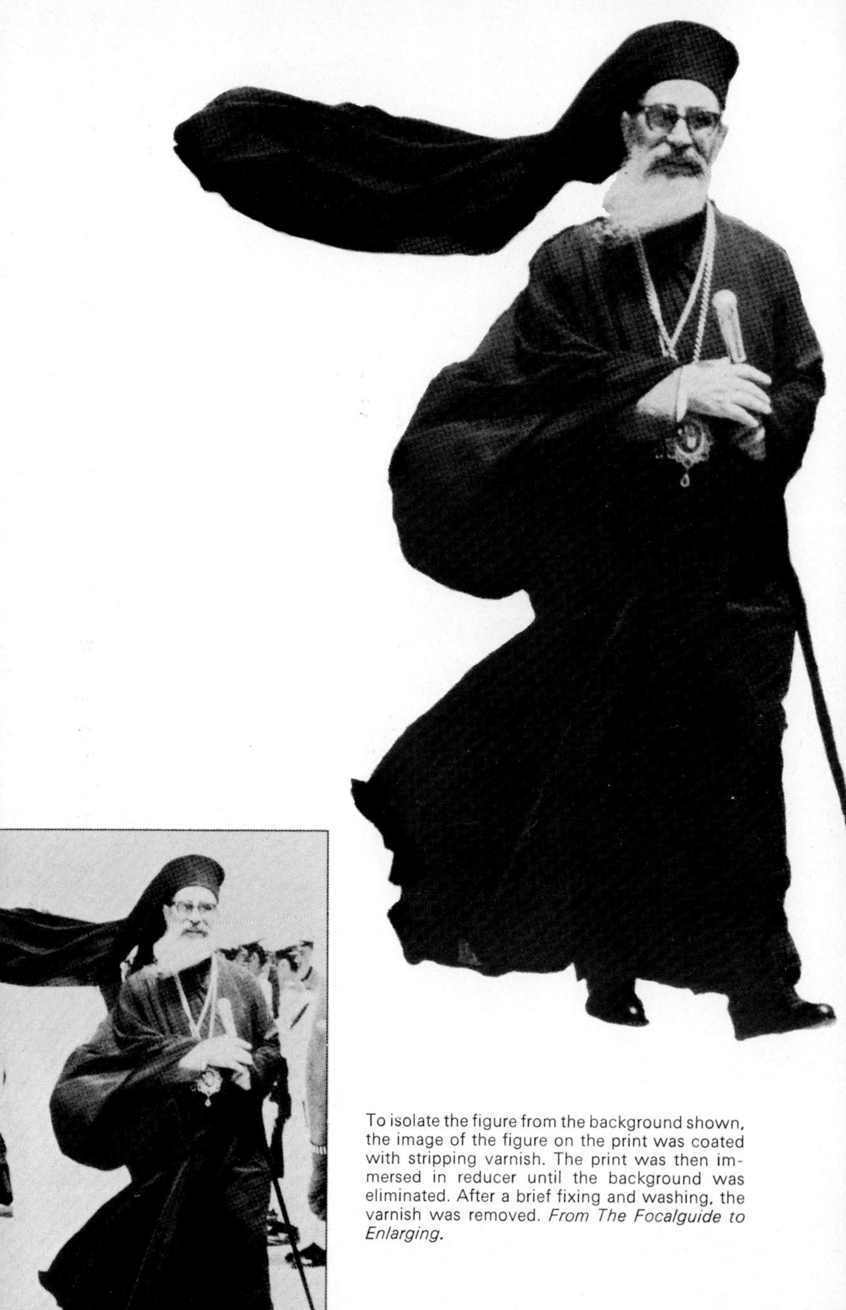

To isolate the figure from the background shown, the image of the figure on the print was coated with stripping varnish. The print was then immersed in reducer until the background was eliminated. After a brief fixing and washing, the varnish was removed. *From The Focalguide to Enlarging.*

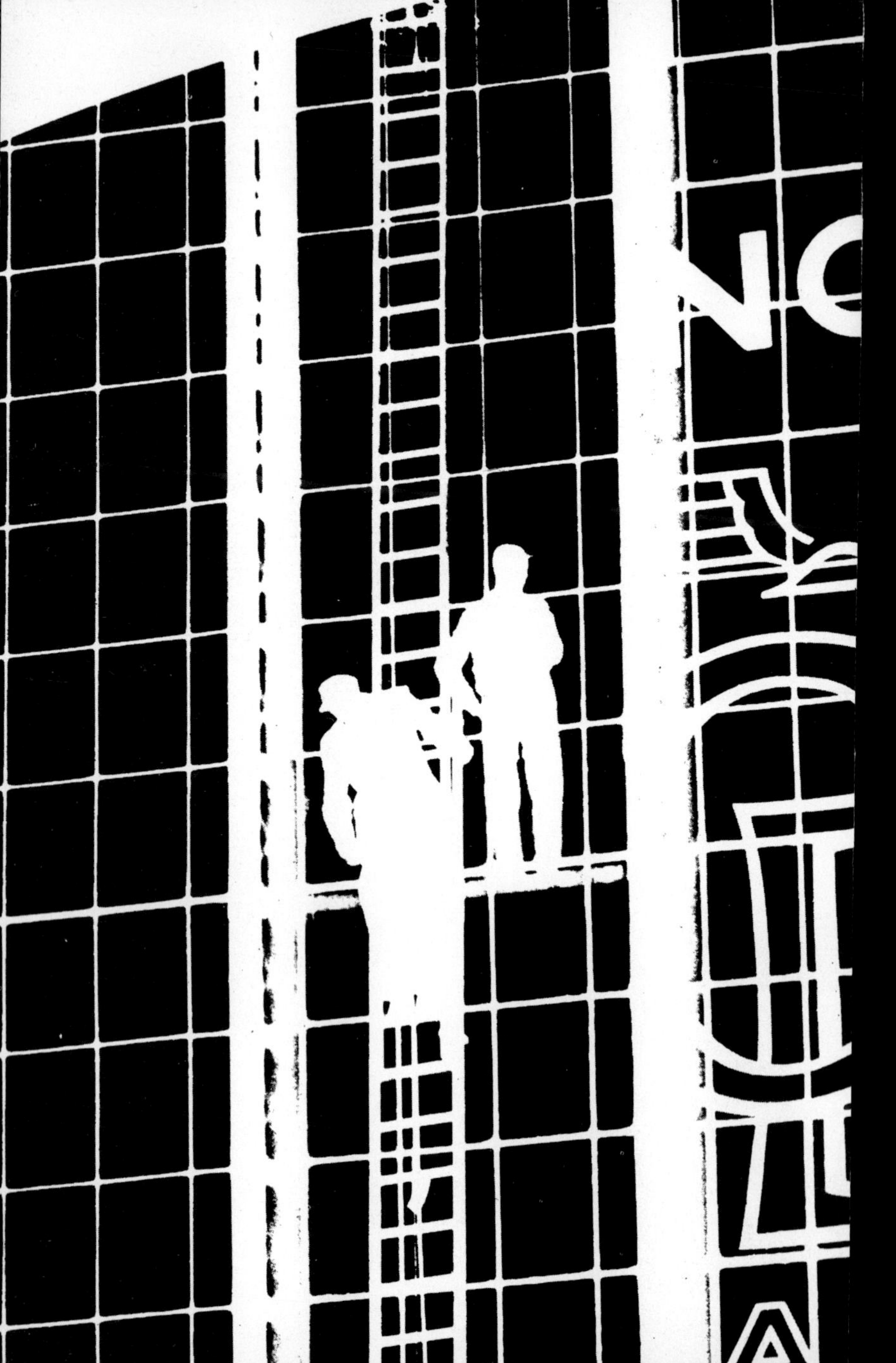

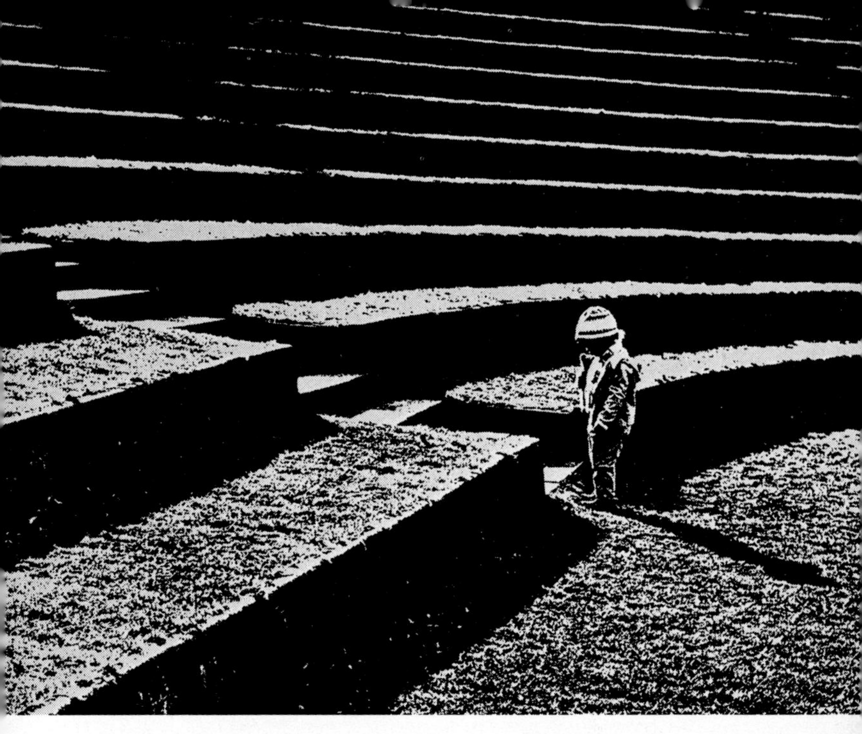

Above: Tricks with the tone range. Some pictorial effects depend on abandoning the natural tone range of the image in favour of various types of compression. Some of these tone modifications can only take place during enlarging. High-contrast abstraction involves duplicating the negative in one or more stages on high-contrast material until all mid-tones are lost and only black and white remain. *Eric Wendelboc; from Enlarging, Jacobson & Mannheim.*

Opposite: Negative print made from a colour transparency. Harsh contrasts are usually preferable in this type of print. *From The Focalguide to Enlarging.*

Pages 108, 109: Combination of identical images or parts of images to produce patterns that do not exist. The top picture uses three prints of the same subject (one laterally reversed) mounted side by side. The bottom picture turns a few trees into a wood by using five prints of the same subject. *Adolf Vrhel; from The Focalguide to Effects & Tricks.*

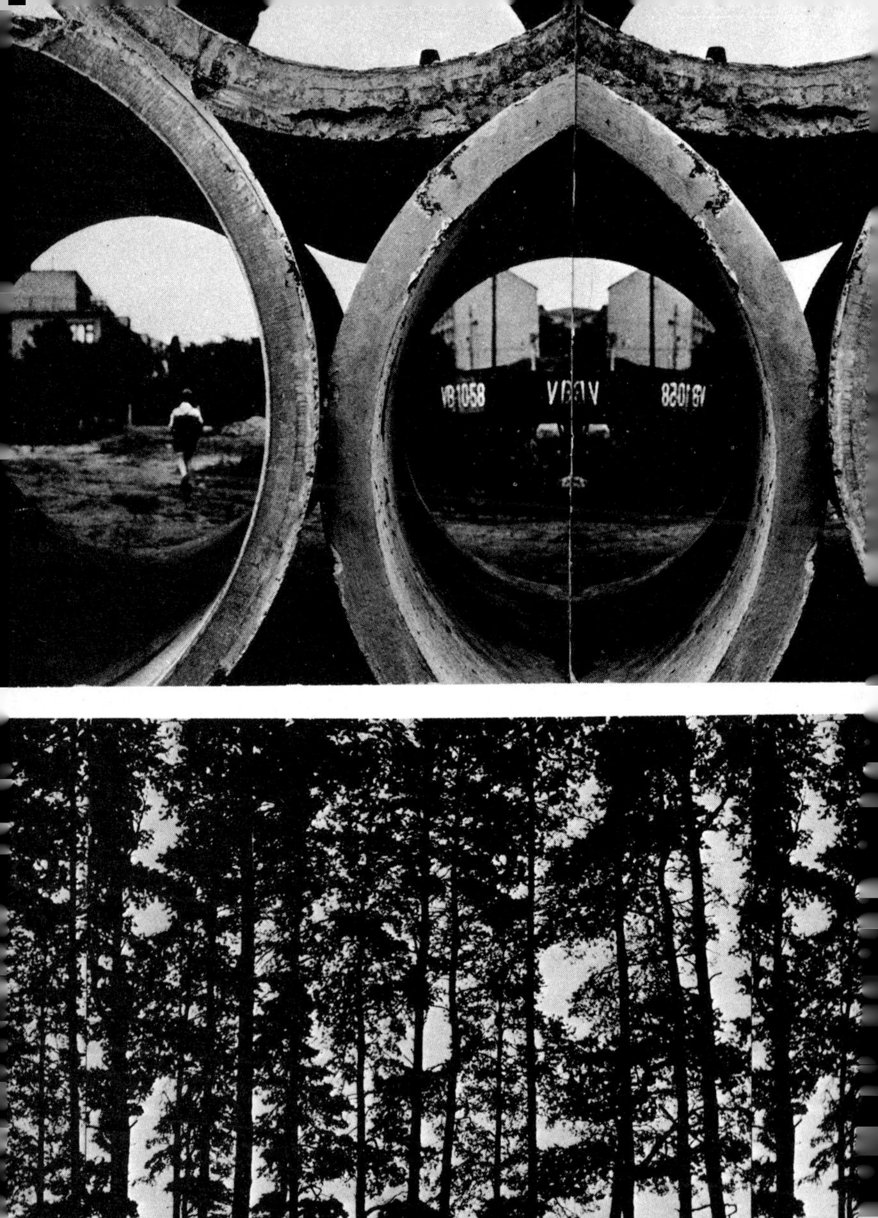
VB1058

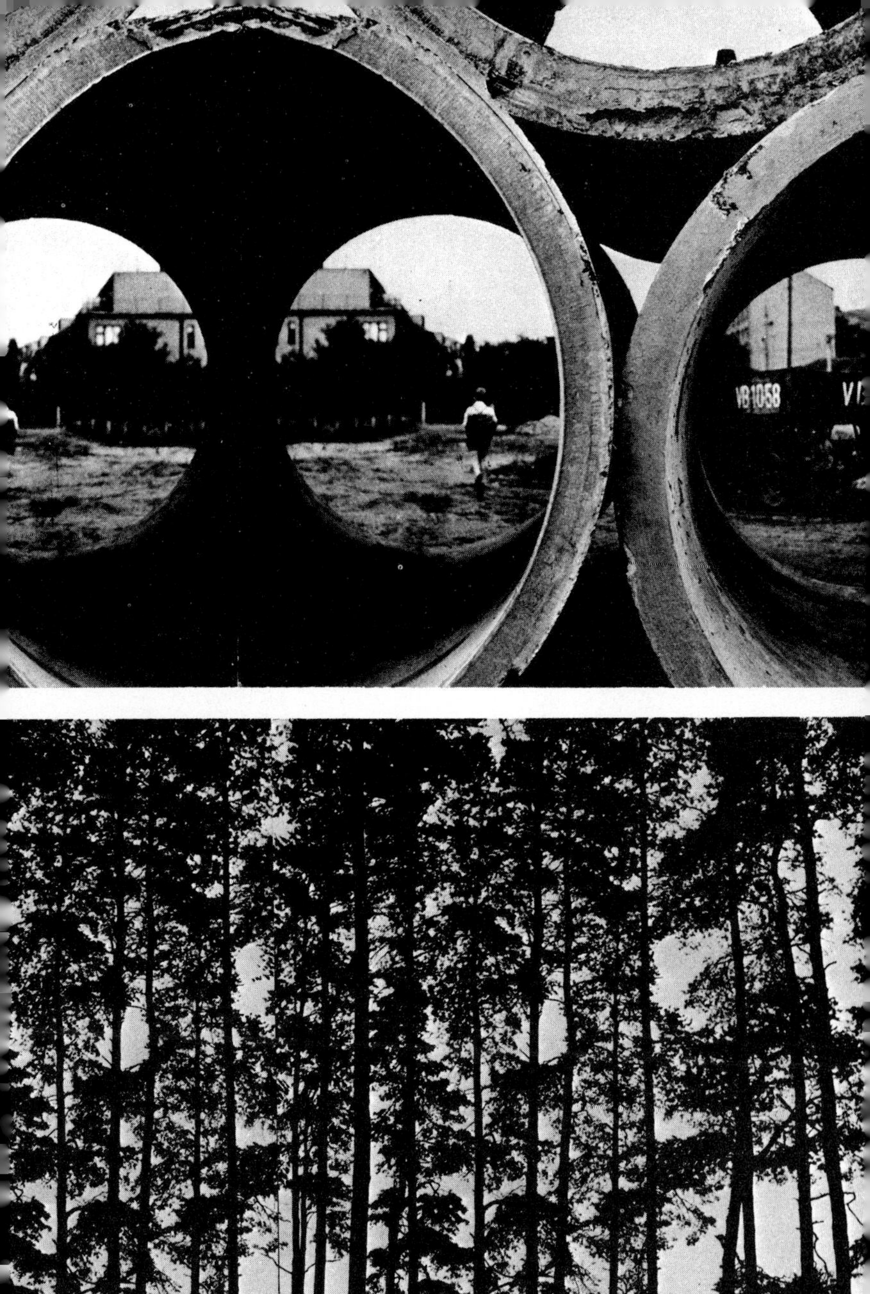
VB1068

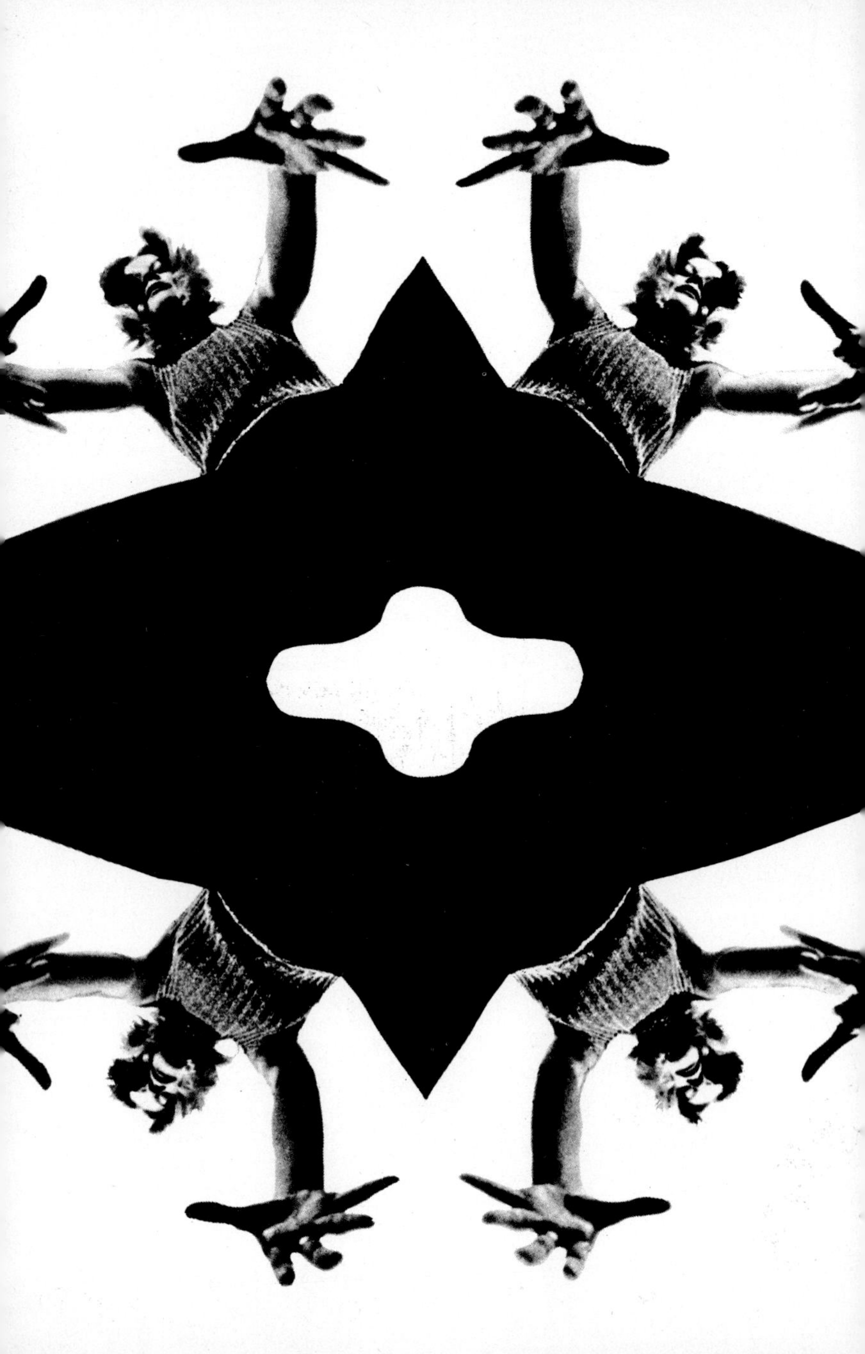

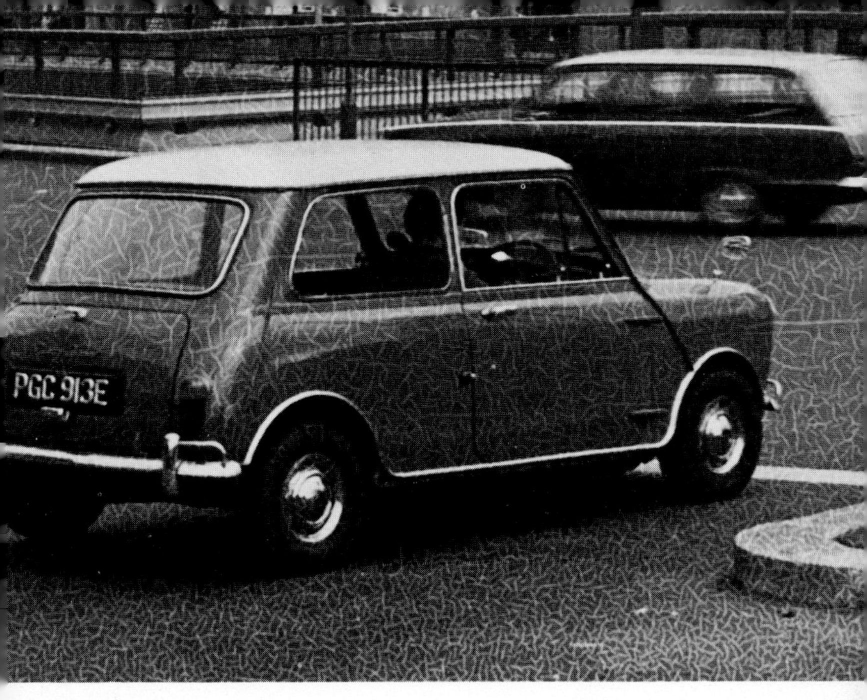

Above: Reticulation is caused by rapid swelling and shrinking of the film emulsion. It produces a characteristic pattern that is sometimes so fine that, in small prints, it can be mistaken for grain.

Opposite: Four prints have been combined from an original taken with a 21 mm lens to provide a startling composition. *From The Focalguide to Effects & Tricks.*

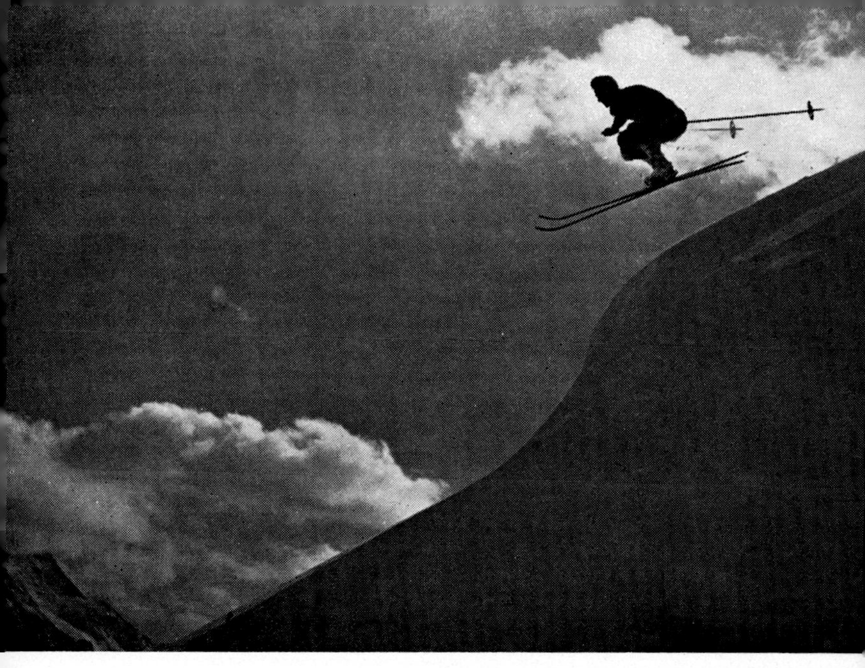

Angling the print. A considerably simpler way of controlling the visual effect of a picture lies in shifting the paper on the enlarger baseboard. Here a slight turn of the paper holder has made the snow-covered slope (*above*) appear appreciably steeper (*opposite*). This treatment is also suitable to improve the impact of portraits, but needs a watchful eye on obvious verticals (lamp posts, buildings etc.) in landscapes. *From Enlarging, Jacobson & Mannheim.*

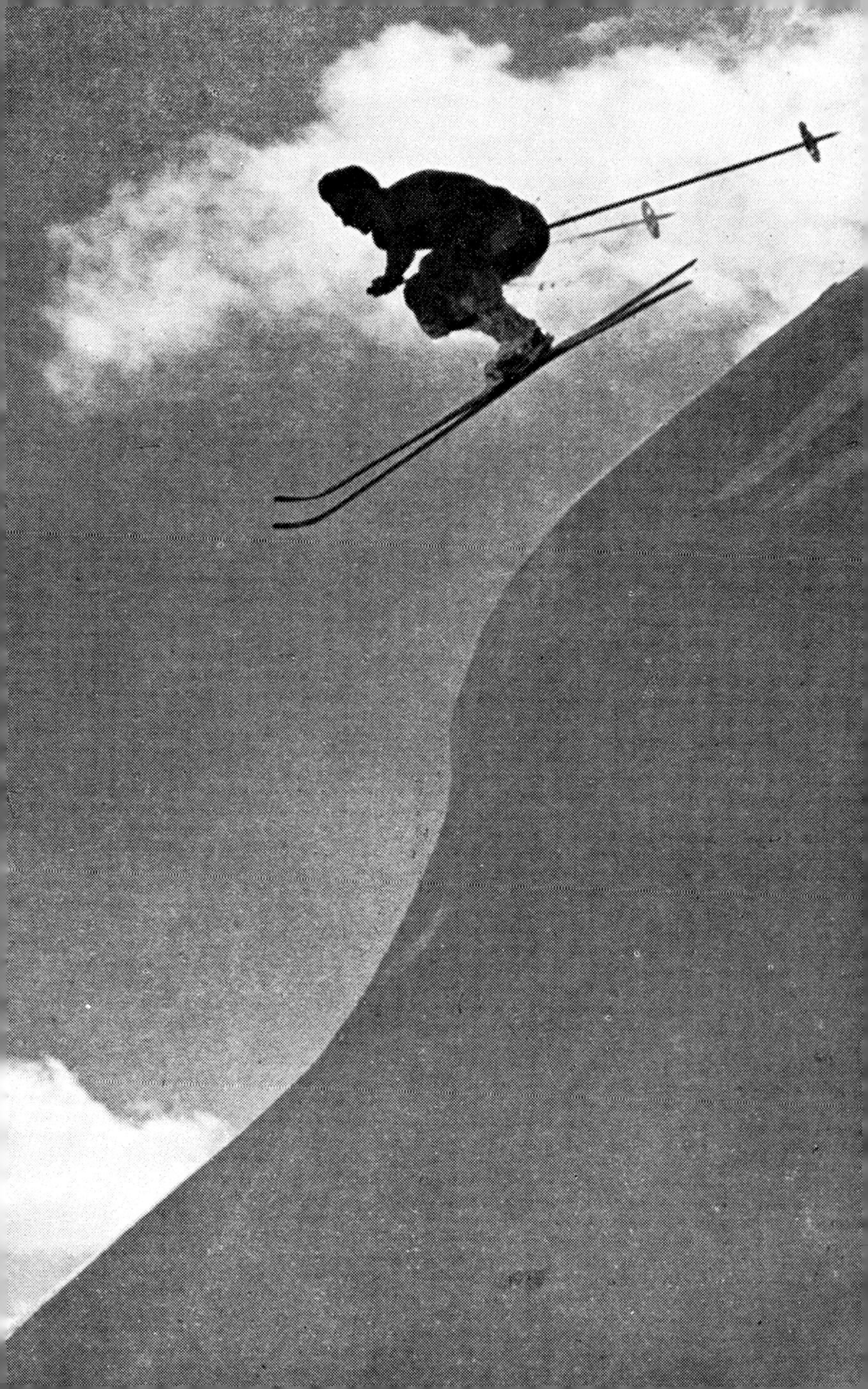

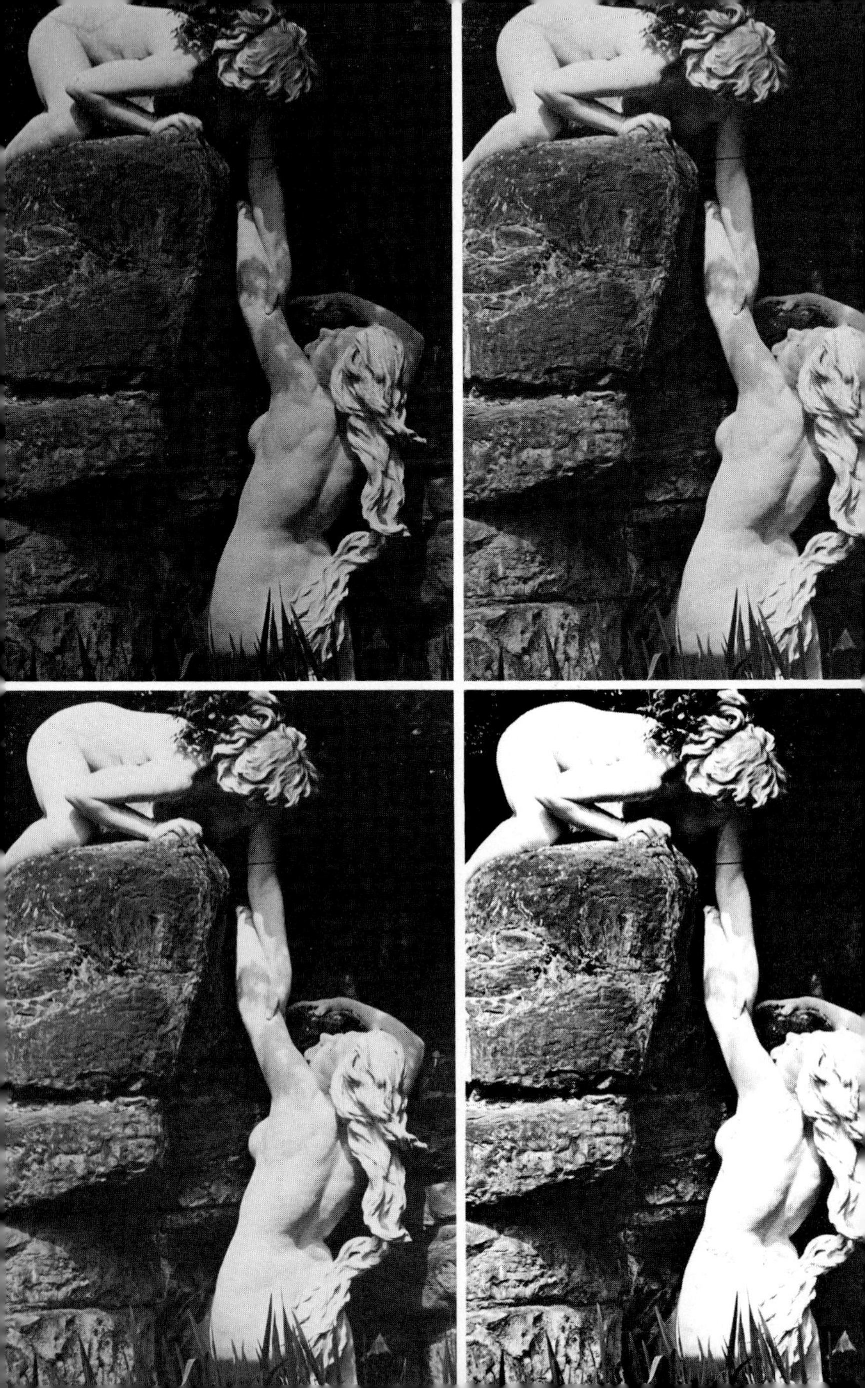

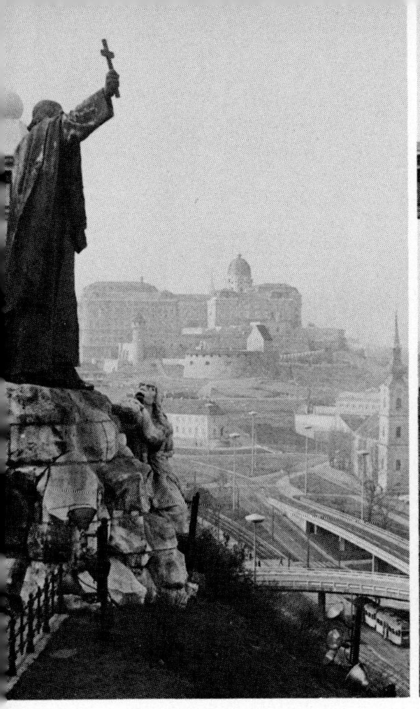
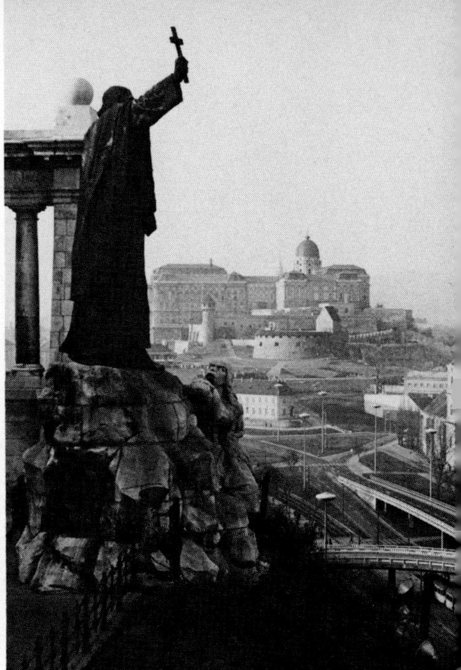

Above: Paper kept too long in storage goes stale (*left*). At best, it acts like paper a grade or two softer, but it can also show unevenness of tone, mottle, streaking, etc. Fresh paper (*right*) gives good differentiation between tones.

Opposite: Most papers are available in four or five contrast grades, from soft to extra hard. The four prints show the effect of printing a rather contrasty negative on Ilfospeed grades, *top left* grade 1, soft or low contrast. *Top right* grade 2, normal. *Bottom left* grade 3, hard or high contrast. *Bottom right* grade 4, extra hard.

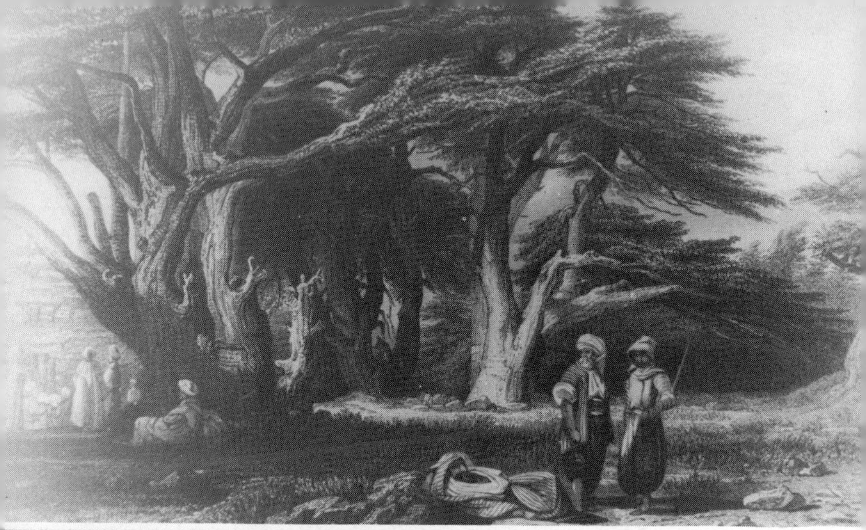

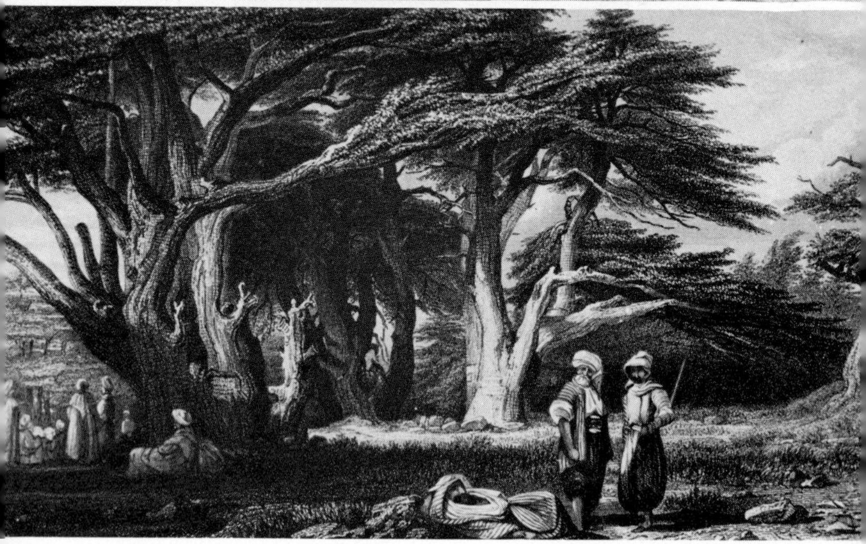

Above: A poor enlarger lens (*top*) may suffer from flare and so reduce image contrast. Uneven illumination and poor definition in the corners are also common faults. The good enlarger lens (*bottom*) resolves fine detail right into the corners and retains highlight brilliance.

Opposite: Print sharpness is subject to various enlarging hazards, even if the negative is sharp. The most obvious cause is faulty focusing; less obvious is enlarger vibration (*right*) caused by unsteady setting up, touching the enlarger during or immediately before exposure, or just walking about in the darkroom while the exposure is taking place.

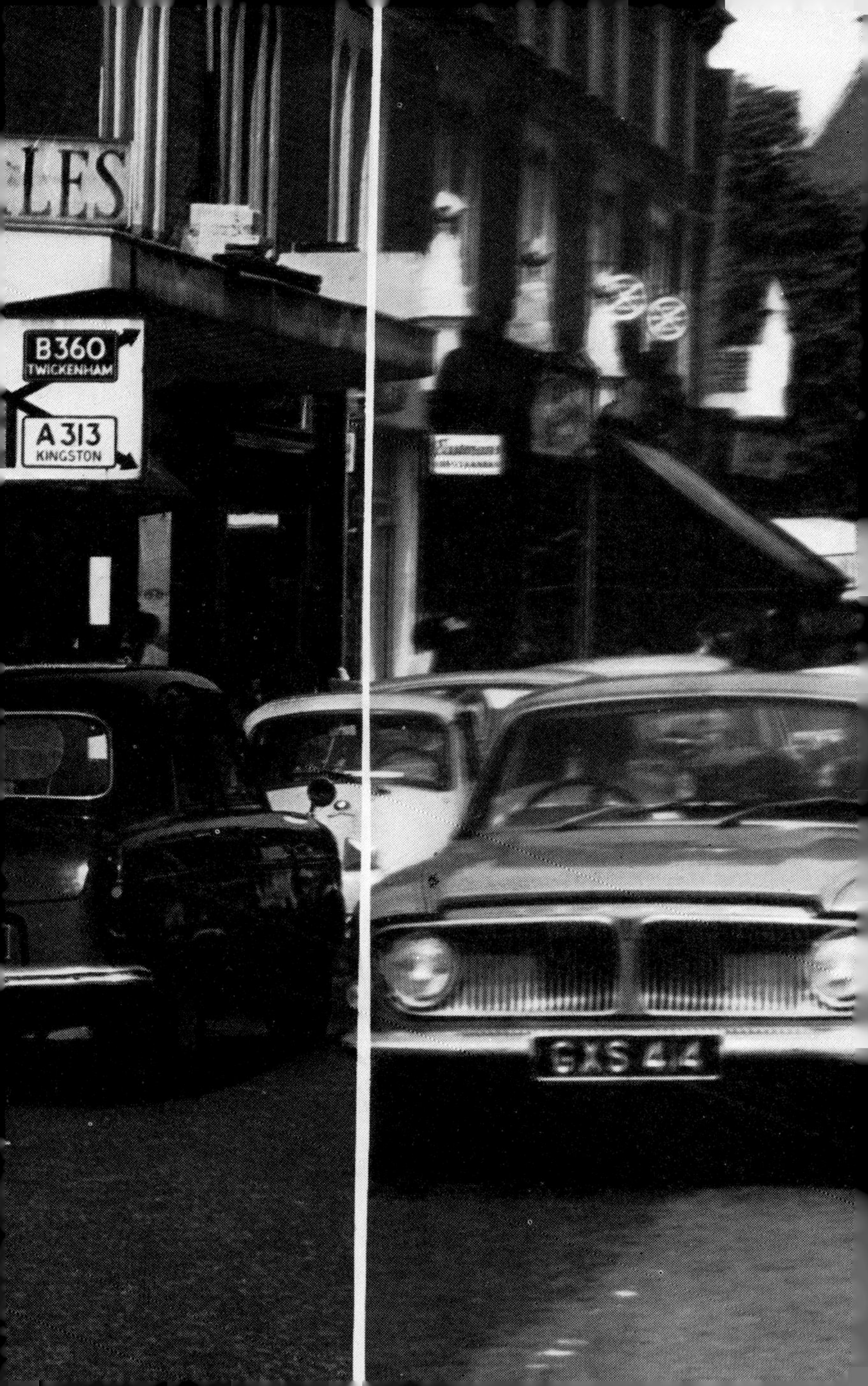
LES
B360
TWICKENHAM
A313
KINGSTON

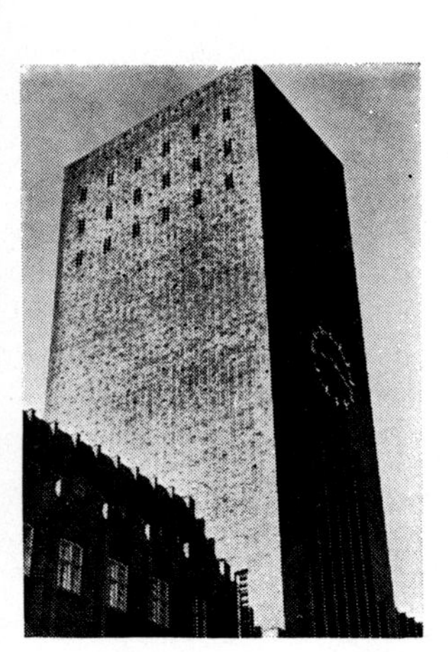

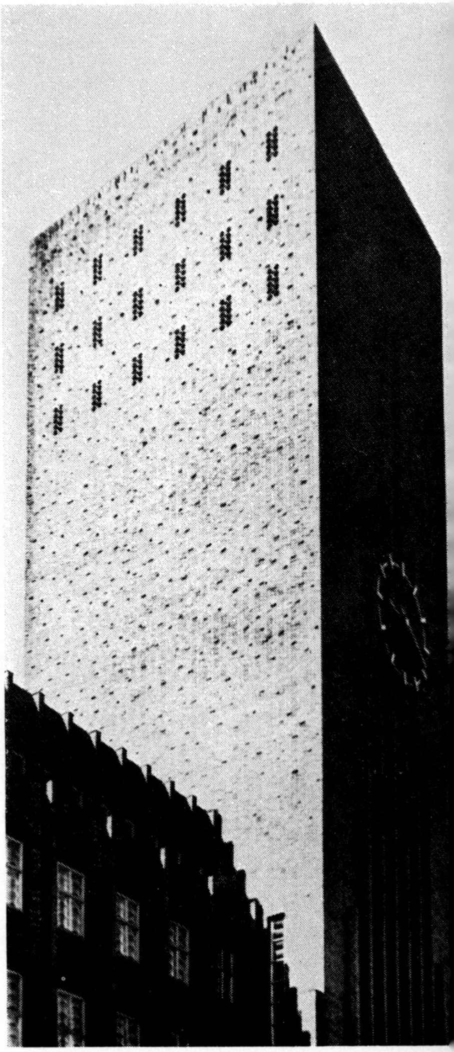

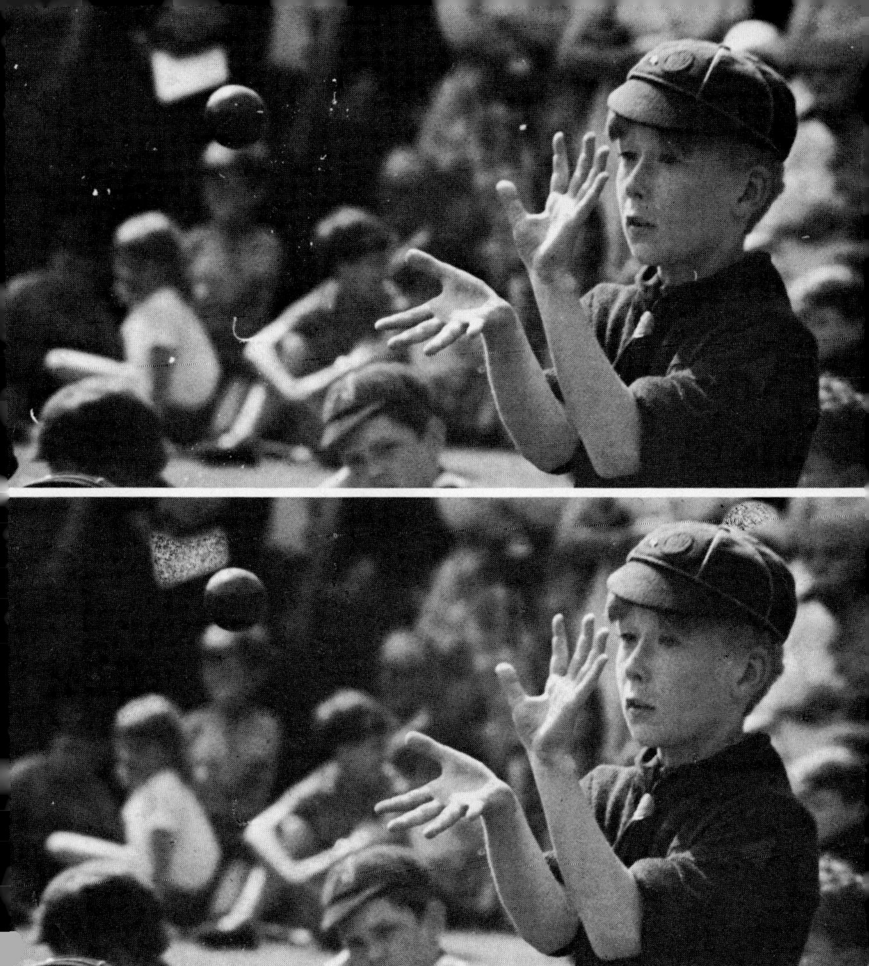

Above: A good sable hair brush, a pot of process black and a steady hand can easily take care of white spots caused by dust on the negative. At the same time, you can often reduce the brilliance of distracting highlights.

Opposite: Correcting converging verticals. In architectural and similar pictures taken with a miniature camera it may be necessary to tilt the camera in order to get the whole of a tall building into the picture. The resulting 'leaning backwards' effect may be corrected to some extent during enlarging by tilting the paper or negative, or both. *From Enlarging. Jacobson & Mannheim.*

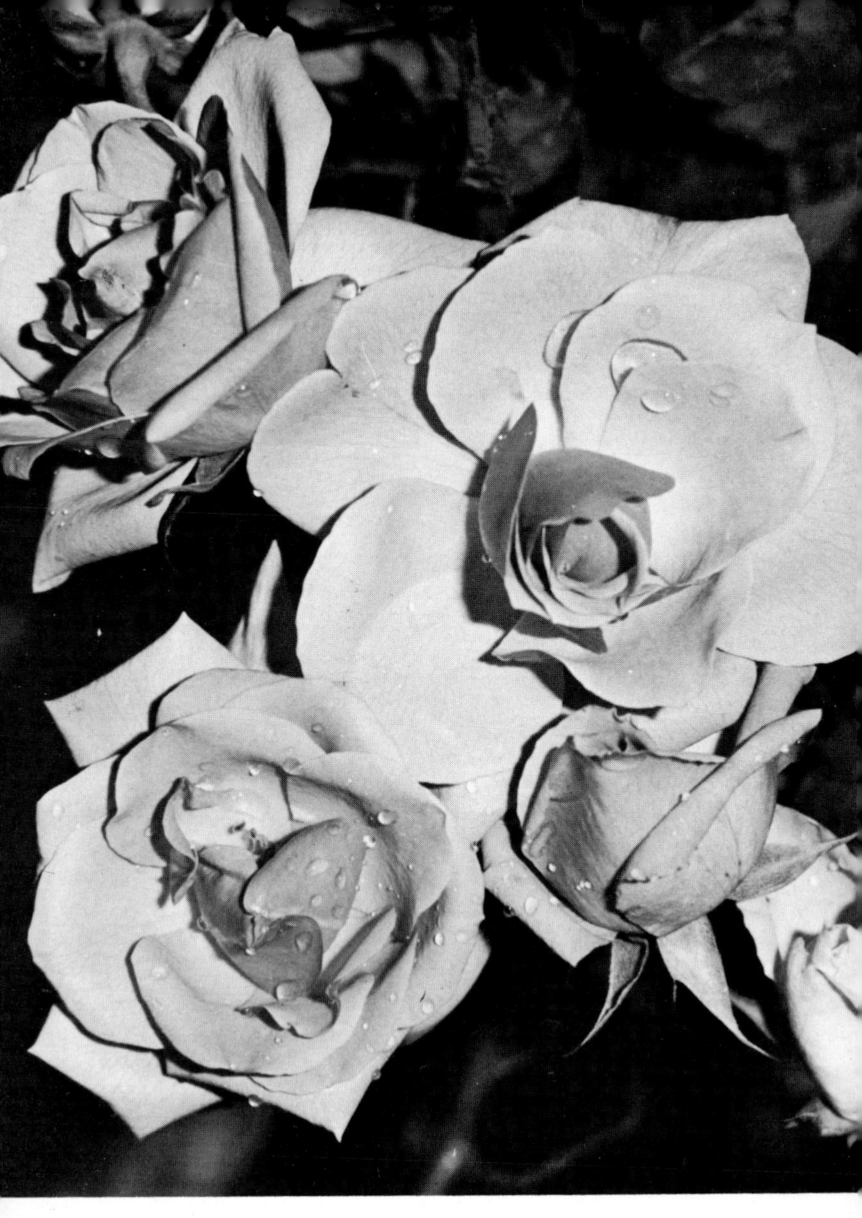

Test your safe light by placing a coin on the paper and leaving it on your baseboard for a minute or two. Then make a print in your normal way.

film loader on the market and they do not cost very much. They are all rather similar in design, consisting of a chamber for the roll of film, light-trapped from a smaller chamber for the cassette connected to a winding handle and a counting mechanism. The cassette chamber is generally arranged so that you cannot open it without closing the light trap between the two chambers.
A short piece of film is left protruding through the light trap and you attach that to the cassette spool, reassemble the cassette and close the chamber. Open the light-tight trap (to allow the film free passage with no risk of scratching) and wind on the required number of exposures (any number you like up to 36). Close the light trap, open the cassette chamber, cut through the film and extract the loaded cassette. It is an easy-to-use relatively inexpensive piece of equipment that can cut your film costs dramatically.

Washing prints

Prints on ordinary bromide paper need to be washed for at least 30 minutes after they come out of the fixer. The fixing process converts unused silver bromide (or other silver halide) to non-light-sensitive compounds that are somewhat unstable but can be washed away in water. Of course, most of them bleach out into the fixer solution, but significant amounts remain. If they are not removed, they will, in time, degenerate and produce stains and other undesirable effects. Single-weight papers are washed clean for all practical purposes after about 20 minutes in running water that is allowed to reach all parts of the print at all times. They should, therefore, be kept separated throughout the washing operation. Double weight prints need 40-60 minutes. Resin-coated papers are effectively washed in five minutes because only the emulsion can absorb solution.
The necessary separation between prints is provided by various designs of print washer. One is a deep open dish with pronounced ribs on the bottom. Water is fed in at force through small jets, so imparting a circulatory motion that keeps prints on the move. Another is box-like with specially-designed separator plates between which the prints are slipped. Inlet and outlet pipes ensure that the water circulates adequately around the prints.

Less expensive and quite efficient is a sink stopper replacement that empties the sink (or bath) when the water rises to a certain level and then allows it to refill with fresh water.
One ingenious method uses a simple syphon tube on a sucker pad to draw away fixer-laden water from the bottom of a dish while fresh water runs in at the top—a system that is quite easy to improvise. This is, in fact, the essential of any washing operation—that the contaminated water should be drawn out and not left to rise to the top of a dish and overflow. Almost any system that takes care of the removal of contaminated water, together with frequent separation of the prints, is quite adequate.

How to buy accessories

It is easy to persuade yourself that every accessory you see is essential. Certainly there are many labour-saving gadgets that are very tempting. It is wise to temper your enthusiasm with a little sensible thought, especially if you are setting up a darkroom for the first time. No matter how bottomless your pocket, there are enough manufacturers of gadgets to find their way down there in double quick time.
We described the essentials in the previous chapter. We have added several inessentials to the list in this chapter. There are plenty more and you could spend a great deal of money equipping your darkroom with just a few of them. It is more sensible, however, to start with the essentials and gain experience with them. Find out which parts of the process you find irksome and cast around for something to make things easier in that direction. Then, as you gain proficiency, look for the items that can actually help you to get better results—and realize how few of them there are. Most accessories are simply alternatives and they are often ridiculously expensive, even when costing comparatively little, for the task they perform.
If your cash is limited, settle for the minimum of equipment and the maximum of materials. You are more likely to get better results from long practice than by fitting your darkroom out with every conceivable luxury.

Print-Making Materials

So far, we have been concerned almost exclusively with equipment. We have had very little to say about the items you will be buying most frequently and on which, in the long run, you will spend most money. These are the actual print-making materials—basically paper and chemicals.

What makes a print

This is not a textbook on photographic printing or enlarging. There is another book in this series—the *Focalguide to Enlarging*—that takes you through the whole process. Here we deal with the basics. A photographic print is produced by passing light through a negative on to a light-sensitive emulsion on a paper, plastic or any other support. For the moment we will refer to paper, even though many so-called photographic papers are now, to all intents and purposes, plastic. The normal printing papers are commonly called 'bromide' papers because silver bromide is a major constituent of their emulsion. You can make a print with the negative in contact with the paper, so producing an image on the paper that is the same size as that on the negative. Or you can project the image on to the paper through a lens—generally to produce enlarged images. Contact prints are now rarely made because most cameras use rather small negatives.

When the light passes through the negative and strikes the paper emulsion it acts the same way as did the light from the subject on the film emulsion. It blackens it selectively in proportion with the light falling on each part. To be accurate, if affects it in such a way that it can subsequently be blackened by treatment with a chemical solution—a developer. Just as the image on the negative is reversed in tone compared with the original subject (because the more the light the blacker the image), so the print image is reversed com-

pared with the negative. It therefore reproduces the tones of the subject.
The paper, by itself, is not enough, just as the film is not enough. The image is invisible until we amplify the effect the light had on the emulsion. That we do with chemicals—a solution containing a developing agent and various other constituents to ensure a clean print with well-graded tonal values.
The developer changes the silver bromide to black metallic silver in the areas where it has been light-struck but has no effect on the areas the light did not reach. In those areas, therefore, the emulsion is still light-sensitive after development. So we need a further chemical solution to destroy the sensitivity of the unused bromide. This is the fixer. It converts the unused silver bromide to substances that are not light-sensitive and the image is then said to be fixed.
The materials with which we are primarily concerned then are paper and chemicals—using the term paper to cover all types of printing material.

Resin-coated papers

The traditional photographic printing material is a high quality paper coated with a light-sensitive emulsion and various other layers to assist adhesion, protect the emulsion from abrasion and so on. The paper base is absorbent. It soaks up the chemicals used in processing much more readily than the emulsion layer and has to be washed thoroughly when processing is complete.
Various types of paper base have been produced to combat the tendency to absorb moisture, including a waterproof-back type much favoured by the armed foces. The latest product, and the only one to be introduced generally, is a sandwich construction with a thin sheet of paper laminated on both sides to a plastic coating. This is commonly known as RC (resin-coated) paper in the Kodak-speaking empire and PE (polyethylene) where Agfa reigns supreme.
The great advantage of such coated paper is that it is almost completely non-absorbent. Only the emulsion, coated on the top plastic layer, needs to be washed. Additionally, it can, with its own special chemistry (shorthand for the processing chemicals and

procedure) be very rapidly processed, sometimes with the assistance of a developing agent incorporated in the emulsion. In the glossy form, it retains a pleasingly high glaze after drying and it dries very flat with only the slightest tendency to curl.
There are those who object to RC paper on the grounds of its lack of tactile appeal, the inferior quality of the image, and possibly the ephemeral nature of the plastic coating. It is certainly strange to the touch, compared with paper, but that is hardly a serious objection. The quality of the image is a highly debatable point that seems to be very near the hair-splitting evasion of the 'will not be convinced' diehard. The possible short life of the plastic coating is a more serious matter. What the truth of that is, we laymen will not know for many a year. What do we know of the lasting ability of photographic paper? Has its discoloration or its ageing effect on image quality been measured scientifically? Has not the plastic coating been subjected to similar premature ageing tests for the same purpose?
For most of us the questions are academic. Our masterpieces are not likely to live for a century or two and, if they do, those that are in colour are more likely to deteriorate because of the inadequacy of the dyes than the short life of the plastic. There are more permanent methods of black-and-white printing for those who need them but they had better hurry up and make their archival prints because their negatives are on a plastic base.
For the average worker, resin-coated paper is a blessing, simply because it considerably reduces the time from enlarger exposure to finished print. It eliminates the necessity for glazing, but is available in other surfaces for those who prefer them. It dries almost perfectly flat in a very short time. Its disadvantages are few, the main one being perhaps that its surface is rather easily damaged when wet.

Paper surfaces, grades and weights

Photographic papers, resin-coated or otherwise, are made with various surface textures and various types of emulsion.
Surface textures are fewer now than they used to be and tend to be confined to glossy, semi-matt and one or two slightly roughened types known, according to the manufacturer's whim, as lustre,

stipple, pearl and so on. These generally have a finely-broken surface of regular or irregular pattern that can work wonders in concealing slight grainy effects but can also obscure fine detail, especially in small prints. They are fine for pictorial work but are not generally favoured for commercial photography that has to be put through another reproduction process. They can be very difficult to rephotograph.

It used to be possible to obtain photographic papers that were off-white or even cream in base colour but they are now becoming rare. More strongly tinted papers—in blue, orange, red, green, etc. as well as metallic gold, silver and steel blue, and fluorescent colours—are available from specialist manufacturers. Various other bases can be obtained, too, such as opal film, washable linen and aluminium. These are particularly useful for display purposes. The opal film looks like any other photographic print when viewed by reflected light but has the luminosity of a transparency when transilluminated. Photo linen can stand up to heavy punishment without effect on the image and can be cleaned to restore its brilliance.

The major manufacturers produce a limited range of papers in the three main types—bromide, resin-coated and stabilization—apart from special products for commercial, scientific and industrial use. The more esoteric products come from specialist manufacturers and are often gathered together by a single agent in each territory.

A type of paper that used to be a great deal more popular than it is now, adds silver chloride to the usual silver bromide in the emulsion and is consequently known as chloro-bromide paper. It is sometimes referred to as an exhibition paper because, with suitable development, it can produce a range of image colours from red-brown to pure black that many exhibition workers find more pleasing than the cold black of bromide paper. The paper was available in a wide range of tints and surface textures but many of these have now been rationalized out of existence. Today's giant manufacturers need a correspondingly huge demand to make any line worth continuing.

The orthodox photographic papers are produced in two thicknesses or weights—single-weight and double-weight. Single-weight is to be preferred for most purposes, if only because it costs less, but some find it difficult to handle in the larger sizes. In fact, some

textured surfaces are available only as double-weight paper in the larger sizes. Resin-coated papers are generally available in one weight only—sometimes called medium weight.
Some papers can be supplied in extra light-weight and airmail versions while the specialist materials—opal film, linen, etc.—are generally supplied in one version only.

Emulsion contrast

Depending on how the film is exposed and processed, negatives may vary in character. One worker may prefer rather thin, flat-looking negatives, another may like to be able to see good strong tones on the film. Or the subject of one set of pictures may be evenly illuminated while the lighting on another occasion may have been so directional as to produce high contrast between shadow and highlight areas. Or the processor may simply make a mistake.
Whatever the cause, negatives vary in density and contrast. Nevertheless, most of them can be printed quite satisfactorily, especially by an expert printer, on the same type of 'normal' paper. For the best possible print, however, it might be necessary to print on an emulsion that gives a rather more or less contrasty image. Consequently, photographic papers are produced with different emulsion characteristics, specified as grades.
Grade 0 or 1 (manufacturers' specifications differ both in number and actual emulsion characteristics) is a soft (low contrast) emulsion designed for use with high-contrast negatives. Grade 5 or 6 is an extra hard (high contrast) emulsion designed for use with low-contrast negatives. Between the extremes is a Grade 2 or 3 that is regarded as normal and intermediate grades that are less or more contrasty.
The normal classification is largely a personal matter because each worker naturally tends to regard the paper grade he uses regularly as normal. In most cases it is Grade 2 or 3, depending on make, because that is the paper intended to be used with the normal mid-density, well-graded negative. The other grades may differ in sensitivity, the more contrasty papers needing more exposure, although at least one manufacturer has succeeded in standardizing the sensitivity over all paper grades except the most contrasty.

Some papers are produced with multiple-layer or mixed emulsions that are designed to respond differently to coloured light. They are used with filters that change the colour of the enlarger light slightly and thereby alter the contrast characteristics of the emulsion. The effect is that you have several grades of paper in one box or packet. When you change the filter, you change the paper grade. These papers have had a chequered career and have never been exceptionally popular in Europe. Those who do use them regularly and have mastered the none-too-easy technique involved, were very unhappy when a major manufacturer discontinued the line. It is said to be coming back in a slightly different form, however, and is worth a trial.

Colour papers

Colour papers work just like colour film. They have three separate emulsion layers, each sensitive to a different part of the spectrum of white light, broadly grouped under red, green and blue. The emulsions incorporate dyes that are released on development to combine in their various layers to produce a full range of colours. The dyes are universally called yellow, magenta and cyan, which are mixtures in light terms of red and green, red and blue and blue and green respectively.

It is as yet impossible to produce dyes in films and paper that are absolutely pure and stable. Variations occur and, when colour printing, we have to filter the light from the enlarger lamp (change its colour) to reconcile the differences. The filters used are consequently also yellow, magenta and cyan and are interposed in the light beam between the enlarger lamp and the negative. When the light is sufficiently corrected, the light passing through the various coloured portions of the negative selectively exposes the three layers to reproduce the colours of the original subject. The filtration is critical and, as we mentioned in the previous chapter, it causes beginners a great deal of trouble.

Prints from transparencies

Until comparatively recently, most colour prints were made from colour negatives on basically the same principles as black-and-white printing. Now, however, there are two forms of colour reversal paper, corresponding roughly to colour reversal film, for printing from colour slides. One is processed in a similar manner to reversal films. A negative monochrome image is first produced, the remaining light-sensitive parts are fogged to produce a positive image and colour-developed to release the dyes. The silver images are bleached out to leave the full-colour positive dye image.

In the other form (Cibachrome) the dyes are already present in the emulsion layers when it is exposed. They are selectively destroyed where they are exposed to light, so producing white or lighter colours and unaffected where the light is weaker, producing black or deeper colours. The main advantage of this method is that it is possible to use more stable dyes. A considerable practical advantage is that, although filtration still needs to be handled with care, there is much greater latitude in the time and temperature of processing.

Resin-coating was first introduced for colour materials because it reduces the risk of cross contamination between the solutions used. Indeed many processes eschewed the use of paper entirely and used a totally plastic base. Most colour materials are now resin-coated, the notable exception being the Cibachrome dye-destruction process, which has reverted to the plastic base with no paper content.

Developing and developers

All print materials have to be developed to produce a visible image. Developing is basically what chemists call a reduction process and the main constituent of the developer solution is accordingly known as a reducer or developing agent. It reduces the light-sensitive silver bromide or other silver halide in the emulsion to non-light-sensitive metallic silver that appears black.

To produce an image of suitable density, the developer has to act on the emulsion for a given time at a given temperature. In film developing, the time and temperature is critical for optimum results but in paper processing quite wide variations are possible. This is because the paper can be exposed in such a way that it can be developed to finality (as far as it will go). With film, this would result in loss of middle tones but the paper emulsion has a much more restricted tonal range (the number of distinct separate tones it can squeeze in between white and black).

Ideally, most black-and-white papers are processed for about two minutes at 20°C (68°F) but no detectable difference is likely to arise with considerable variations in both factors—provided the exposure is correct.

Similarly, there is less scope for producing widely-differing types of developer for papers. Film emulsions vary in sensitivity and grain structure. They intend to include slightly larger grains of silver to form the image in faster films. Papers are very much less light-sensitive than films and their emulsions do not have to pay much regard to grain size. The image on the paper is never enlarged; the enlarged grain structure of the negative is always greater than that of the print.

A few developer formulations have been produced but the choice of developer is neither critical nor gives the average photographer much concern. Whereas he might be very reluctant to process a film in any developer other than his own favourite brew, he will generally accept any paper developer at a push. Most of them are based on simple formulae that have stood the test of a great many years. The main choice is between those sold as powders to be mixed with water and those sold in concentrated liquid form to be diluted for use.

Colour papers are different in that they are, with the one exception already mentioned, very dependent on the correct time and temperature of development and they must be processed in their own particular chemistry. The main reason for that is that they have to maintain a balance between the three separate emulsions. Only at a critical level of development can the three emulsions remain in step to produce correct colour. An additional increment of exposure may have a different effect on each of the three layers. There are also considerable differences in emulsion chemistry that make solutions suitable for one type of paper totally unsuitable for another.

This selectivity is offset to some extent by the fact that some manufacturers use chemistry so similar that substitute solutions can be produced by independent companies to process more than one make of paper, perhaps with slight variations in time and temperature; or with the aid of separate additives.

Fixing solutions

The developed black-and-white print is still sensitive to light, as we have already explained. The unused silver halides have to be made insensitive to light and this we do by immersing the print in a fixing solution, so-called because it preserves the image. The first photographs suffered from the fact that an image could be produced but it could not be made permanent.

The fixer—often called hypo—converts the silver halides into compounds that are no longer light-sensitive and are soluble in water. They can still be harmful to both image and paper base so they have to be washed out.

Fixing solutions are traditional in formulation and there is no need to cast around for the ideal brew. There are two types, one faster acting than the other, but the use of the faster type for paper is rather pointless because papers fix much faster than film—about 30 seconds in ideal conditions and two minutes in general practice. Again, however, there is the choice between powders and concentrated solutions.

Mixing your own solutions

For the regular darkroom worker, there is undoubtedly money to be saved in making up your own black-and-white developer and fixer from raw chemicals. For the irregular worker, it is hardly worth the effort. He is likely to waste more chemicals than he uses. The formulae shown here are suitable for all normal photographic papers.

MQ BROMIDE PAPER DEVELOPER

Metol	1.5
Sodium sulphite anhydrous	25
Hydroquinone	6
Sodium carbonate	30
Potassium bromide	2

Water to make	1000
Dilute 1 + 1 for use	

PQ BROMIDE PAPER DEVELOPER

Sodium sulphite anhydrous	50
Hydroquinone	12
Sodium carbonate anhydrous	60
Phenidone	0.5
Potassium bromide	2
Benzotriazole	0.2
Water to make	1000
Dilute 1 + 3 for use	

The quantities indicated are proportions. Any unit can be used. Grams per litre is the most convenient. Benzotriazole can be replaced by about 35 ml per litre of IBT Restrainer or similar commercial antifoggant. Phenidone is Ilford's alternative to metol.

When making up the MQ formula, dissolve a pinch of the sodium sulphite first in about three-quarters of the total volume of water at about 45°C (120°F). Add the rest of the chemicals in the order shown, stirring constantly but not too vigorously to avoid beating in air. When all the chemicals are totally dissolved, make up with cold water to the total volume.

The pinch of sulphite is designed to prevent early oxidation of the metol. You must not add too much because metol will not dissolve in a strong sulphite solution. Phenidone presents no such problems and the formula can be made up by mixing the chemicals in the order shown.

Most fixing solutions are acidified to arrest development immediately and contain a hardener to protect the emulsion from subsequent damage. Neither is particularly necessary for prints if you develop to finality and pass the developed print through a water rinse or stop bath before fixing. The function of the stop bath is to reduce or eliminate the alkalinity of the developer remaining in the print and so preserve the life of the fixer.

The straightforward fixing solution consists of about 100-150 g of sodium thiosulphate in a litre of water. You can acidify it if you wish by the addition of 25 g of potassium metabisulphite. Such a

solution, provided its temperature is above 10°C (50°F) fixes a print in a minute or two if it is fresh and the prints are not simply dumped in it in a pile. They must be kept moving and separated.
The hardener is completely unnecessary. It helped a little with hot glazing but is more of a hindrance than a help with any other form of afterwork. This does make it unnecessarily expensive to use proprietary fixers for papers because they are virtually all acidified and contain hardeners.

Buying printing materials

Each worker is confident that the particular brand of printing paper he uses is the best, which is as it should be. The best paper for you is that which gives the results you want. There is nothing to choose in quality between the established brands but there may be characteristics of surface texture, colour, sensitivity and even feel that make you prefer one brand to another. Naturally, price could come into it, too, but there seems to be little competition in that area. You can buy job lots of paper from certain dealers at bargain prices and they are always worth trying.
If you do a lot of experimental printing (to use a polite term for mucking about in the darkroom) or otherwise make a lot of prints that need not be of superlative quality, some of these special offers may well interest you. It is very unlikely that the product will be outright bad and if the dealer is well established, it will probably be worth the price asked. But you must compare the quality of your results with those on fresh paper to make sure that you do not accept inferior quality because you know no better.
Economy in the buying of materials is important to most of us but the economies must be in the right direction. If you find that you are not always printing in standard sizes, choose your paper size carefully. You might be able to settle on a larger size that cuts handily to two sizes that you commonly use. Strangely, cutting larger paper to a convenient number of smaller sizes without waste does not seem to pay very well since the introduction of metric sizes. Quoting from an outdated price list for example, 25 sheets of 20.3 × 25.4 cm (8 × 10 inches) paper cost 1.71 (the currency does not matter for purposes of comparison). This would cut to

100 5 × 4 inch sheets. That size is not available but 100 sheets of 10.5 × 14.8 cm (4.1 × 5.8 inches) cost only 1.89. It hardly seems worth cutting it yourself. The A4 size does cut directly to two A5s or four A6s but is available only in 100-sheet boxes. There are some larger sizes, however, that are available in packets of ten sheets and could prove useful if you have a cutter that can handle them.

Storing the paper

Having bought the paper, you have to store it and you may have to store quite a lot if you have no dealer near at hand whose prices are reasonable. We have already mentioned the value of an old refrigerator for this purpose but it is worth emphasizing that the greatest enemy of printing paper is damp. It does not mind cold at all. In fact, it flourishes on it and deteriorates faster in a warm atmosphere, particularly if it is also humid. Damp can lead to a lot of unpleasant activity in the emulsion, resulting in uneven development, lack of contrast and even damage from papers sticking together. Resin-coated papers are a little less prone to these troubles because at least the paper is protected but they can still give a lot of trouble. If your darkroom is at all damp, wrap all your paper packets and boxes securely in cling film or put them in sealed polythene bags. Always keep them inside their original black envelope, which affords quite a lot of protection.

Silica gel and other drying agents can be used in your paper cupboard but do not rely on them exclusively unless you use the type that indicates when it needs drying out. Do not use a paper safe or even a light-tight drawer where dampness is present. The essence of these is that the paper is unprotected and it is not easy to make a light-tight drawer that is immune from damp.

Buying and storing chemicals

Make up your own chemicals if you do a lot of printing or buy them in the larger quantities that are now easily obtainable. Using commercially-produced concentrated solutions is said to be an expensive way of buying water but there are some highly-concentrated solutions that make up to considerable quantities. Study the prices and quantities carefully and decide what is best for your purposes.

It is generally more economical to make up your developer from two-powder packs. These, too, are available in very large sizes that work out a great deal cheaper than a 500 ml bottle of semi-concentrate, the price of which is becoming absurd.

Be careful when making up solutions from powders (particularly fixing solutions) and preferably do not do it in the darkroom. If a little powder floats about in the kitchen or bathroom, it will do little or no harm to anybody: in the darkroom it can be a menace. You never know where it is going to settle, but there is a 'law' that says that it will not be somewhere harmless.

Similarly, watch the drips when you pour chemicals. Store them in wide-mouthed containers if possible. They have less tendency to slurp and shoot the contents over the edge of flask or dish. For large containers, you can buy dispensing taps that are a perfect safeguard against this trouble, while even small bottles can be fitted with pouring tubes.

Pour from the opposite side to the label, assuming that you have remembered to label your made-up solutions. An obscured or soaked-off label does not lead to even-tempered working conditions in the darkroom.

Store large containers on the floor unless you have built a stout support to hold a cubitainer, for example, with a tap. Smaller bottles are reasonably safe on the shelf above the processing dishes. It is not generally advisable to store chemicals in the same cupboard as papers but that need not be an absolute law in these days of improved packing and wrapping materials. Sealed packets of powders, for example, should be perfectly safe as should securely stoppered bottles but give the papers the added protection of cling film or bag wrapping if you are in any doubt. As a general rule store chemicals in this way only when there is no other option, such as shortage of space, or when the darkroom is very damp. Although powders should be safe in their plastic bags or sachets, the outer wrappings are often very susceptible to damp that can work its way inward.

Processing Film

When you are ready to start processing and printing your own films, the starting point is the exposed film you have just taken out of the camera. Black-and-white film processing is the simplest of all the tasks confronting you. It is purely a time and temperature process—rather like putting a cake in the oven.

The necessary equipment is a developing tank, a thermometer, two measuring beakers (at least) and two film clips. The materials are the film, the developer, fixer and water.

Loading the tank

You start in the darkroom with the roll or cassette of film and the developing tank. At this stage the white light is still on. Take the lid off the tank and extract the spiral. Lay the parts to hand where you can easily locate them when you put the lights out. Lay the film beside them. Switch out all the lights (*no* safelight) and remove the end of the cassette or break the seal on the rollfilm. Extract the film from the cassette, winding the knob a few turns to tension the film and so loosen it in the cassette, if necessary—or detach the rollfilm from its paper backing.

From now on, be careful to handle the film by its edges only. Load it into the spiral according to the manufacturer's instructions. This is a nerve-wracking job on the first few occasions but try to keep calm about it. Sweaty palms are no help at all. This is where you are glad you made a good job of the blackout but are somewhat frustrated at being so completely visually detached from your arms.

It is not a good idea to use a film with unrepeatable shots on it for your first attempt at loading a developing tank. In fact, this is the ideal time to use a film to take those lens-testing or suchlike shots that you have been meaning to take ever since you bought the camera. If you make a mess of the loading, you are no worse off than when you started.

When you have managed to get all the film into the spiral, put the spiral in the tank and replace the lid securely. Now you can turn the lights on again.

Preparing the developer

The procedure naturally depends on what type of developer you are using but it generally involves pouring solution from a stock bottle of developer into a measure marked in fluid ounces or millilitres (cubic centimetres for practical purposes). If you use a concentrated solution calling for 50 ml or less to be measured, use a beaker of that capacity or not more than 100 ml. Having measured the required amount, pour it into a larger beaker (500 or 600 ml) and add water from the cold tap to the total quantity recommended for your tank. If the cold tap water is exceptionally cold, you might add slightly warmer water instead.

Suspend the thermometer in the solution. A plastic spring clothes peg is useful for this job if the thermometer makes no provision for it. Check the temperature. In temperate climates and depending on your storage conditions it will more often than not be lower than the 20°C (68°F) generally recommended for black-and-white films. Fill a smallish basin, pan or other receptacle with hot water to make a water jacket. Stand the container of developer in it until the thermometer registers the required temperature. Give the developer an occasional swirl to keep it mixed and speed up the warming.

If you are working in a very cold darkroom (and you should avoid that if possible) it may be necessary to warm the developing tank, especially a metal one, at the same time. You can use the same method, but keep the water below the lid-to-body seal. They are not always completely watertight. Alternatively, just before the next step, you can pour clean water at 21°C (70°F) into the tank and leave it there for one minute before completely draining it out. If you do that, however, you may find that you need to adjust the recommended developing time.

Processing the film

Check the manufacturer's leaflet for the developing time of your film and pour the developer into the tank as quickly and smoothly as possible. At the same time, start the timer or check the time on watch or clock, preferably with a sweep second hand. Immediately start agitation of the developer. That is now usually by inversion of the tank slowly and deliberately but some older models have a twiddle stick down the middle for twisting to and fro. Agitate continuously but gently for 30 seconds and then give two or three slow inversions or twiddles at one-minute intervals.

Between times, prepare your fixer solution, in a different beaker, just as you did your developer. If you have to spend some time getting the temperature right, prepare the fixer before you pour in the developer. On the other hand, do not worry too much about its temperature. Anything from 15-21°C (60-70°F) is suitable.

At the end of the development time, pour the developer out of the tank into its beaker for subsequent return to its stock bottle, or pour it away if it is a one-shot type. Fill the tank with water at 15-21°C (60-70°F), invert it once or twice and pour out. Pour in the fixer and agitate for about 30 seconds. Subsequent agitation is not necessary. At the end of the fixing time (follow the manufacturer's instructions) pour out the fixer and rinse the tank again. You can then look at the film, handling it very carefully by the edges only, to make sure that there is something on it before you bother to wash it.

Temperature variations and reticulation

The rinse water between solutions, the final wash water and the solutions themselves should, ideally, be at the same temperature. Marked differences can cause rapid swelling and shrinking of the emulsion that leads to a crazing effect of tiny cracks known as reticulation. This is generally barely visible on the negative but becomes very apparent on enlargement.

Unfortunately, there is little or no consistency in this effect. It may depend to some extent on the type of water used. It appears, however, that modern films are highly resistant to reticulation.

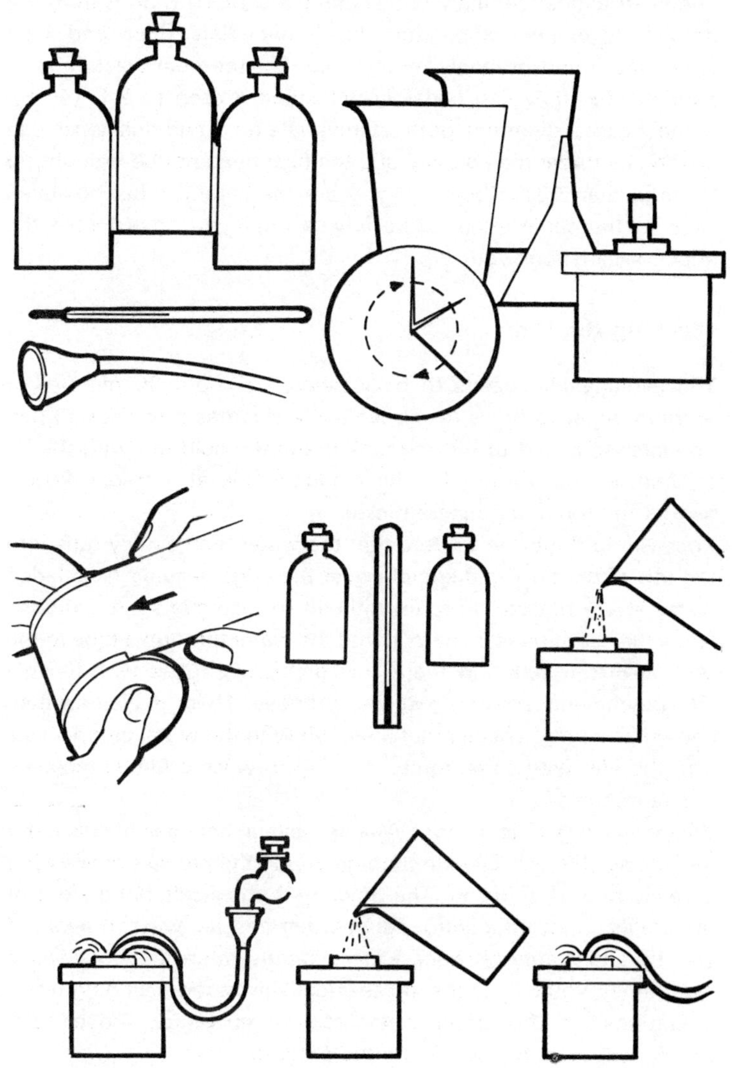

To process films you need storage bottles, measuring flasks, funnel, developing tank, timer, thermometer and wash hose.
The procedure is: Load film into tank; check solution temperatures; pour in developer; pour out and rinse; pour in fixer; pour out and final wash.

They can almost certainly withstand a 6°C or 10°F drop from the normal developer temperature for intermediate rinse and fixer temperature and probably much more. For the final wash, after a hardener-fix, they can certainly withstand a drop to 7°C (45°F). In most cases, therefore, both intermediate rinse and final wash can be directly under the cold tap and the fixer need not be brought up to more than 13°C (55°F). If you are the careful type, however, stick to the same-temperature advice until you have tested the effect of variations yourself.

Washing the film

The average film needs to be washed for about 20 minutes in running water to be as near chemically clean as it is likely to get. The easiest way is to put the tank under the cold tap with the lid off and let the tap run for the required time at a steady flow—neither full force nor a mere trickle.

You will no doubt be advised that the water then simply runs into the top of the tank and straight over the edge, leaving fixer-laden water at the bottom. It is not difficult to disprove such a theory. Nevertheless, it does no harm to run the water through a tube to the bottom of the tank and there are commercial tubes with flexible tap attachments sold for just that purpose. There is also an item known as a turbo washer that mixes air with the water and delivers it to the film with some force, claiming to wash a film completely in five minutes.

Where running water is not available, several changes of still water are just as efficient. Even in running water, the process of washing is really one of diffusion. The unwanted chemicals diffuse out of the emulsion into the surrounding water and are washed away. If you fill and empty the tank at five minute intervals about six or eight times, you will do the job as effectively as most running water operations. In this case, water at a temperature above 13°C (55°F) will probably accelerate the process.

Many claims are made about washing methods, times and temperatures—some of them designed to sell equipment. If you want to test your own procedure, you can buy something for that, too. There are indicator solutions that you can use on a piece of waste film or paper to show whether you have achieved the required chemical-free state.

Colour film processing

There are two types of colour film—negative and reversal, also known as print and slide. Colour negative film is the easier to handle and, with the improved chemistry of recent years, processing is hardly any different from that for black-and-white film.

The main important difference is in the temperature of the solutions. A popular independent two-bottle system, for example, is used for all Type II colour negative films with a total processing time (excluding the final wash) of about seven minutes, but it has to be used at 38°C (100°F).

The procedure is broadly the same as that we have described for black-and-white films with the exception that, at such high temperatures, pre-heating of tank and film is a necessity. After loading the film into the tank, therefore, you fill the tank with water at 40°C (105°F) for one minute. You then drain the water out completely and pour in the developer at 38°C, agitating for 20 seconds and then four times a minute over 2¾ minutes.

Pour out the developer for re-use and give three 15-second rinses in fresh water at 35-40°C, or you can use an acid stop bath for 30 seconds. Next comes a bleach-fix solution at 35-40°C for three minutes followed by a final wash at 30-35°C for five minutes. Your film is then ready to dry for printing.

A few variations in the procedure are possible but the minimum developer temperature is 35°C (95°F), so you need a thermometer that reads rather higher than the average type and it must be reliable, because the developer temperature is critical.

This type of processing, and there are several such products, has brought colour negative processing well within the capabilities of any reasonably careful person. It is not inexpensive but compares well with the least expensive commercial charges and is, of course, a great deal more convenient.

Reversal film processing is a different story. This, too, has been simplified over the years but it is still a tedious job and really only worth while for the dedicated do-it-yourselfer. Apart from the rather long task of processing, you have to buy slide mounts, cut the film and mount each exposure if you intend to project them. On top of that, of course, the most popular 35 mm colour reversal film cannot be home-processed.

There are four basic steps in reversal film processing, the extra steps being necessary because it is an indirect process. The image is not produced directly by the camera exposure but by a subsequent fogging (by light or chemicals) of the silver halides not affected by the camera exposure. Hence, you first develop the film in a more or less normal manner to produce a negative image. You do not want this image but you have to develop it to render it insensitive to the subsequent fogging step that activates the remaining halides. This second lot of light-struck halides is then colour developed to release dyes in the three emulsion layers in proportion with the colours and densities of the original image (because they are in inverse proportion with those of the negative image).

Finally, a bleach/fix removes the silver image and stabilizes the colours. Rinses or more prolonged washes are required between each step. There is nothing difficult about the process but many find it tedious and barely economical compared with commercial processing prices. However, as processing prices are soaring, you may decide to try it.

Because you have no further chance to manipulate the image (as you do when printing from a negative) processing times and temperatures are extremely critical. Even small variations can alter the density, contrast or colour of your transparencies.

Cutting and filing

Slides are almost universally mounted singly after processing or, in the larger sizes, placed in acetate or similar sleeves that allow them to be viewed without removing them from their protective covering.

Negatives have a further process to undergo before they become viewable so they have to be preserved in a usable state. With most enlargers, it is preferable to handle negatives in strips—four or six 35 mm, three or four 120s. Single 35 mm negatives, in particular, are very tricky to handle.

The most popular 35 mm filing aid is an envelope or bag to take strips of six, generally open at one end. Such bags can be bought loose in hundreds or can be incorporated in wallets, loose-leaf folders and other filing aids. In those cases the bags may be open along one long edge instead of at the end. It is certainly advisable to use something of this sort to preserve your negatives. The one-time practice of rolling up the whole 20 or 36 exposures and cramming them into a film can is definitely not to be recommended. It is not a lot better to keep the whole film (six strips or more) in one envelope. Constant insertion and extraction will eventually lead to scratches and other blemishes. Stick to one strip per envelope if possible.

Most such envelopes are made from translucent acid-free paper that enables you to view the contents with some difficulty. You can also obtain clear acetate versions which, although more expensive, make the contents more readily accessible and can even be printed through for proofing purposes. Whatever you do, do not put your negatives in envelopes or other wrappings not specifically designed for the job. Many ordinary papers contain ingredients that can harm photographic emulsions.

Filing the negatives in such a way that you can easily find them again is a terrible problem for most people. Subjects tend to vary widely on a film and even on a single strip. How do you file a strip containing three shots taken at the zoo—one of a child eating an ice-cream, one of the giant gorilla and one of a passing aircraft? The filing genius knows the answer but really efficient filing means a lot of work and a meticulous mind. If you do not like the one and cannot cultivate the other, probably your best bet is to file in chronological order. You may have a rough idea when you took that particular shot you are searching for.

If being able to find a particular negative years afterwards is important to you, then your shooting must be disciplined with that fact in mind. Waste film rather than carry out two or three different assignments on the same roll. Do not leave film in the camera when a particular job is finished. Resist the temptation to take the odd shot of an unrelated subject unless it is really worthwhile.

However you file them, keep your negatives away from the old enemy—damp—and from excessive heat. Most indoor locations should be adequate. If you have an outside or loft darkroom, it would be better not to keep your negatives there unless it is well insulated or you have an airtight box, cupboard or what-have-you. A bag or two of silica gel in the cupboard or container will do no harm.

Black and White Printing

Printing is a much more exacting process than developing the film. It is not difficult, of course, to produce a print of sorts, but good printing is a skill and the best photographic printers are people of immense skill born of long experience.

The object of printing, which is now virtually synonymous with enlarging, is to produce the best possible positive image from the negative image on the film. Generally, that means a print that retains as many as possible of the individual tonal values of the negative and shows a clear white and a true black somewhere in the image. The first sign of bad printing is a muddy greyness where there should be black. The most frequent cause is too much exposure and too little development.

If you have already tried making your own enlargements and have come up with prints that lack sparkle, try a simple experiment. Adjust your exposure time until you can leave the print in the developer for at least three minutes without it going too dark. You will probably be surprised at the improvement in your print quality. Over-developing a print (with the correct exposure) rarely causes problems. Underdeveloping is invariably bad practice.

Setting up

We have already described the equipment you need for black-and-white printing. To start work, set out your dishes in the order: developer, rinse, fixer. Whether you work from left to right or right to left depends on your personal preference and perhaps on the layout of your darkroom.

Pour the required quantity of developer into its dish. It is false economy to skimp on the developer. Put enough in the dish to be able to submerge the print without difficulty and to keep it submerged without constant prodding. Pour a generous quantity of water into the second dish to serve as intermediate rinse and finally pour fixer into the third dish, again not skimping on the quantity.

The developer should be at 15°C (60°F) or higher. The rinse and fixer can be at virtually any temperature but preferably not below 13°C (55°F). If your darkroom is cold, you can place the developer dish in a larger dish containing water at about 20°C (68°F). Keep a thermometer in the developer dish and top up the warm water if the temperature falls significantly. Alternatively, there are various types of aquarium thermostatically-controlled heaters that serve to keep the water at the required temperature indefinitely. Dish-warmers can also be obtained. These are a sort of hotplate on which you stand the processing dish. Some models are also thermostatically controlled.

With the dishes in position, place one set of print tongs by the developer dish and one by the rinse. Place a bucket, bowl or other receptacle with clean water to receive the finished prints and store them for the final wash. You are now ready to make the first print.

Making test strips

To produce a successful print, you must know how long to expose the paper to the projected image. Too much exposure and the print is too dark; too little and it is too light.

Place the required strip of negatives in the enlarger negative carrier and adjust it to frame the negative from which you wish to print. Set the enlarger lens to full aperture. Set your masking frame or cut a piece of white paper or card to the size of the paper on which you intend to print. Switch off the white light and switch on the safelight. Raise or lower the enlarger head to give an image roughly the correct size and then focus it accurately. You may need to adjust the size again and refocus. You will not be able to use all the paper or include all the image unless you have cut the paper to the correct size. There are various negative sizes and papers are made in a compromise range based more on stationery sizes than photographic needs. Move the frame or baseboard paper about until you settle on the composition that pleases you. When you are satisfied, switch off the enlarger lamp.

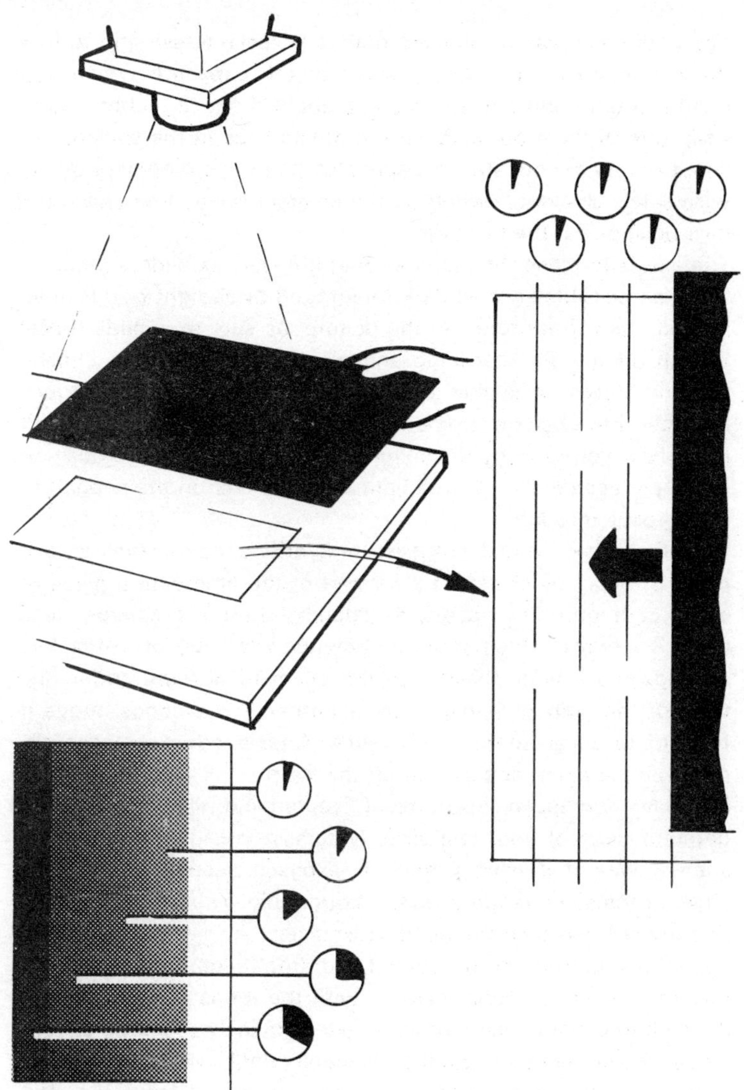

Use a reasonably large piece of paper to make a test strip and place it so that it includes as many tones as possible. Switch on the enlarger lamp and give stepped exposures by moving a black card into the beam. Process the strip and determine by inspection under white light which part received the correct exposure.

The traditional way to proceed now is to make a test strip to find the correct exposure. Take a sheet of the paper on which you intend to print and cut it into strips about 5 cm (2 inches) wide. Keep one of them out and put the others back in the packing for later tests. With your strip of paper clutched to your body or otherwise safely shielded, switch on the enlarger briefly and check the best position for the test strip.

The aim is to place the paper so that it covers as wide a range of tones as possible—not all dark foreground or all light sky. If there are important flesh tones in the picture, be sure to include those. Switch off the enlarger lamp and place the paper in the chosen position. You may be able to do all this by swinging the enlarger's red filter into position. Some people like them, some do not, but they allow you to study the image at greater length and to position the paper accurately. The red light has no effect on the paper, but never focus through it.

Now the idea is to make at least three different exposures on this piece of paper by shielding it for part of the time with a piece of black card or other opaque substance. Stop the enlarger lens down by two or three stops and switch the lamp on. After five seconds move your shield into the beam to obscure about one third of the strip of paper. After a further five seconds, move it forward to cover another two-thirds. After another ten seconds, cover all the paper and switch off the lamp.

You have now given exposures of five, ten and twenty seconds to different parts of your test strip. Naturally, you use the shield in such a way that each differently-exposed section contains as close to the same range of tones as possible. You do not obscure first the sky and then the middle distance.

Take the strip from the baseboard and drop it emulsion side down into the developer. Hold it down with the tongs and gently rock the dish to cover all parts of the paper as quickly as possible. Turn it over and continue to hold it down gently until it will stay down by itself. Rock the dish slightly now and again and leave the strip in the developer for *at least three minutes.* At the end of that time take it out of the developer with the developer tongs and allow surface developer to drain back into the dish.

Drop the strip into the rinse water without allowing the tongs to enter it. With the fixer tongs, paddle the strip about in the rinse for a few seconds, drain it and place it in the fixer. Push it down and rock the dish to submerge it.

After 30 seconds or so in the fixer, you can turn on the white light and examine the strip. With luck, you have one or two bands that are too dark or too light and one that is nearly right. What you are looking for is a full range of tones, providing the subject had such a range—and it should have for your first test. You do not want pure white where there should be some detail or a muddy grey representing a deep shadow or even the pupil of an eye. On the other hand, you do not want the shadows to be jet black along with some of the slightly less dark tones that should show detail.

If all the bands on the strip are too dark or too light, take another strip and start again, opening up the lens one stop if the strip was too light and closing it one stop if it was too dark. Keep the times the same if possible.

If you find that the 10-second strip was a little too light and the 20-second strip a little too dark, try another strip with about 13 and 17 second exposures. After two tests at most, you should have the correct exposure.

Making the print

All you have to do now is to take a full size piece of paper, position it in the masking frame or in the same place as your baseboard paper (by safelight only, of course), turn on the enlarger lamp for the time ascertained and process the paper.

You need not necessarily develop for three minutes this time. The recommended time for most papers and developers is 1½-2 minutes. You should find that two minutes gives you results indistinguishable from three minutes because the aim is to develop the paper to finality and, with the correct exposure, it will develop to finality in two minutes. If you develop your test strip for only two minutes, you cannot be sure that, although the print looks good, it is really fully developed. If you develop a little longer, any tendency to overexpose shows up because the print goes darker, which it would not do if it were correctly exposed and developed to finality. After an excessive length of time it might start to 'fog' when the developer finally attacks the unexposed halides but it will not do that in three minutes or probably even four or five, depending on the paper and developer.

The longer development time, even for the actual print, is a useful habit because it ensures that you do not overexpose and drag the print out of the developer before it is fully developed.

Improving the print

We have described the procedure for printing on a normal grade of paper from a perfect negative, ie, a negative that has no extremes of contrast and is neither too thin nor too dense. With practice, you can produce that type of negative on most occasions but you will inevitably have to handle unsatisfactory negatives from time to time.

You might, for example, shoot a subject in low, even lighting conditions that fool your exposure meter. You give a long exposure but it is not quite long enough. The shadow areas are almost clear film with just a trace of the detail that you really wanted to bring out more strongly. Even the medium tones are a little weak and the densest highlights are far from opaque.

That is the classic underexposed negative, lacking in contrast and very difficult to print. If you try to print it on a normal grade of paper, the print comes out flat, grey and uninteresting. You can improve matters by using a harder (more contrasty) grade of paper, say Grade 3 or 4 instead of your normal 2 or 3.

On the other hand, you may err on the side of overexposure in brilliantly sunlit conditions. Then the important highlight areas (as opposed to tiny brilliant spots in which no detail is required) are practically opaque. The medium and shadow tones are also darker than they should be but not in proportion with those clogged highlights. When you try to print that on the normal grade of paper you have to give a very long exposure to bring out the detail in the highlights but then the medium tones and shadows print too dark. A softer, less contrasty grade of paper might help, say Grade 1 or 2.

Even changing to a different paper grade may not solve such problems. In fact, it rarely does produce a first class print from a poor negative. What you really want is more exposure in the highlights than in the shadows. That you can arrange without too much trouble.

It is self-evident, for example, that if part of the paper is shielded from the image-forming beam during the exposure, no image will print in that area. If you remove the shield part way through the exposure, the image prints less strongly where it was shielded. After all, that was just what you did with your test strip. Thus, you can shield (or shade) any part of the image that a full exposure would cause to print too dark while allowing the rest of the image to form normally. Alternatively, you can shade the major part of the image and allow a small piece to burn in.

The technique is relatively simple. To shade a small portion inside the borders of the image, you cut a small piece of black card, generally in a circular or oval shape and affix it to a wire just thick enough to hold it horizontally. During the exposure you interpose this dodger in the light beam so that no light reaches the area you wish to print lighter. Position the dodger a few inches above the baseboard to avoid a sharp outline and let it tremble slightly throughout the operation so that the wire support does not cast a shadow.

To burn in, take a large piece of card and cut a small hole through which you can direct light on to the area that needs extra exposure while shielding all the rest of the image. Again, keep the card moving slightly to avoid forming a hard edge between the differentially exposed areas.

If the area that has to be shaded is at the edge of the print you can do away with the wire and simply hold the piece of card in the appropriate position, or you can even use your hand.

You can determine the different exposures required from your original test strip or by making further tests for each area. The first-class printer uses these techniques frequently. Photographic paper cannot reproduce all the tones in a good negative and some manipulation is nearly always necessary to produce the best possible print. The difference between you and me and the first class printer is that he simply appears to wash his hands over the print, directing light here and there with casual expertise while we struggle with our bits of card and wire. Practice makes perfect, however, and maybe you, too, will soon graduate to that state of professionalism.

Drying the print

We have described print fixing and washing adequately in the chapter on print-making materials. After the final wash, however, your print may need further attention.

The first problem comes in drying. Ordinary photographic printing papers tend to curl strongly toward the emulsion side as they dry. Straightening them out is relatively easy when you know how but can lead to unfortunate accidents if you are careless. The easiest method is to hold the print diagonally over the edge of a table. The sharper the edge the better. Grasp the protruding corner firmly and pull downward while holding the face of the print flat with the palm of the hand. Be careful that large prints do not curl inward as they reach the edge. That puts in an irremovable crease. Repeat the operation for each corner and the print should then have a slight reverse curl that will straighten later.

If you find such a method beyond you, try drying prints under pressure. Again, there is a simple method. Get hold of sheets or books of photographic blotting paper (a special pure fluffless kind). Interleave your prints with the blotting paper and weight the pile down with suitable objects—not books: the damp will get through.

Heat-drying with a dryer-glazer can be satisfactory, provided you do not use too much heat. The slight curl tends to straighten out as the prints cool.

Resin-coated papers give far less trouble in this respect. They dry very quickly and almost perfectly flat because the paper is coated on both sides with a plastic layer that resists the pull of the drying emulsion.

Glazing the print

For normal purposes, the print is finished when it is dried and suitably flattened. If it is on glossy paper, glazing improves its appearance. Dryer-glazers, as already mentioned, are not too expensive but are not all that efficient either. It is generally said that

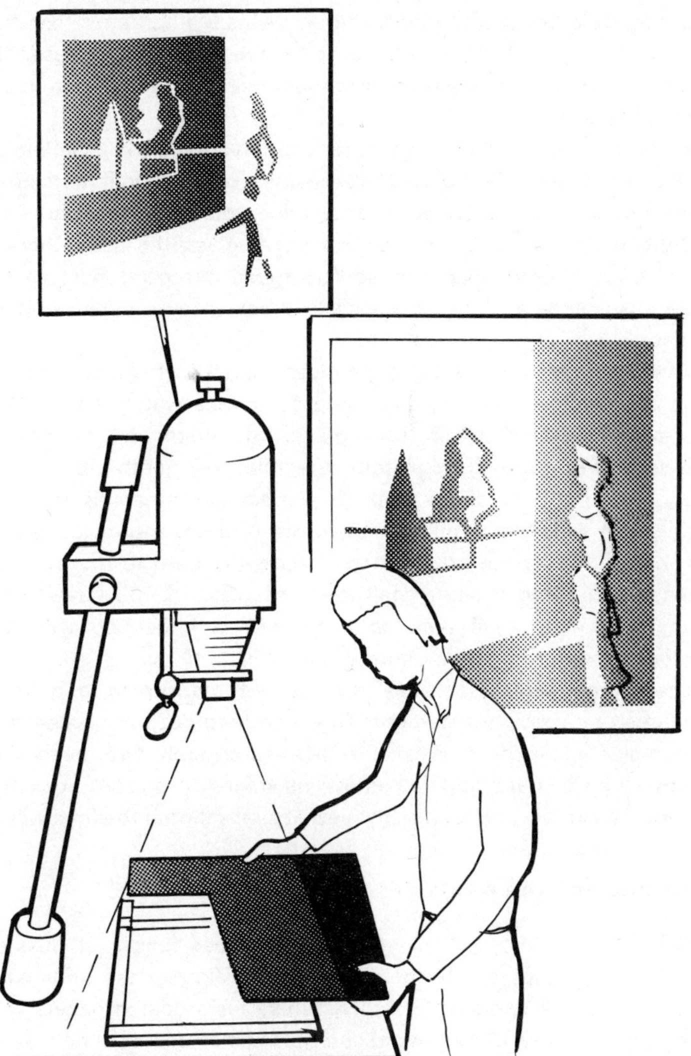

You can shade a part of the print during enlarging so that the required portion prints more strongly without overprinting elsewhere. Use your hands or a piece of card to intercept the light beam. If the area requiring shading is within the print borders use a piece of card on thin wire and keep it moving gently during the exposure.

prints glaze better after hardening in a suitable hardener-fixer but the logic of that is a little difficult to follow. It is probably based on the possibility of damage to an unhardened emulsion if too much heat is used.

You do not have to heat glaze or even have a glazing machine. A sheet of spotless plate glass (more likely to be thick float glass now, in fact) gives a far superior glaze once you get it working. The difficulty is that the print may stick to the glass. If it does, there is no way out but to soak it off and try again. It is worth persevering because repeated glazing seems to break in a suitable sheet of glass.

The art of glazing is to affix the glossy surface of the print to the spotlessly clean glass by excluding *all* surface water and air. It is best to float the paper on to the glass under water and then to use a good, free-running roller squeegee relatively gently on blotting paper on the back of the print. Do not squash the emulsion on to the plate with heavy rolling. All you want to do is to make perfect contact all over the print surface. Leave the print to dry in room temperature and it should fall from the glass. If you have to do anything more than pick an edge with a fingernail, you will probably ruin it by attempting to pull it off.

There are various solutions sold to aid glazing–from a 'cold enamel' to a simple detergent. They can help but the greatest aid is clinical cleanliness. Wash the glass thoroughly after every use with soap or detergent to remove all traces of grease. Soak the print thoroughly and preferably glaze it straight from the final wash.

Retouching the print

However careful you are, you may find that specks of dust or minute scratches on the negative have disfigured the print with white or black spots or lines. If you use resin-coated papers you must be extra careful to avoid such blemishes because the plastic coating does not respond well to the removal of black marks.

On ordinary paper, black marks are relatively easily removed (with practice) by knifing, the most suitable instrument being a razor blade, single-sided if you can find one. The idea is to scrape away the offending blackened emulsion. If you work very, very slowly

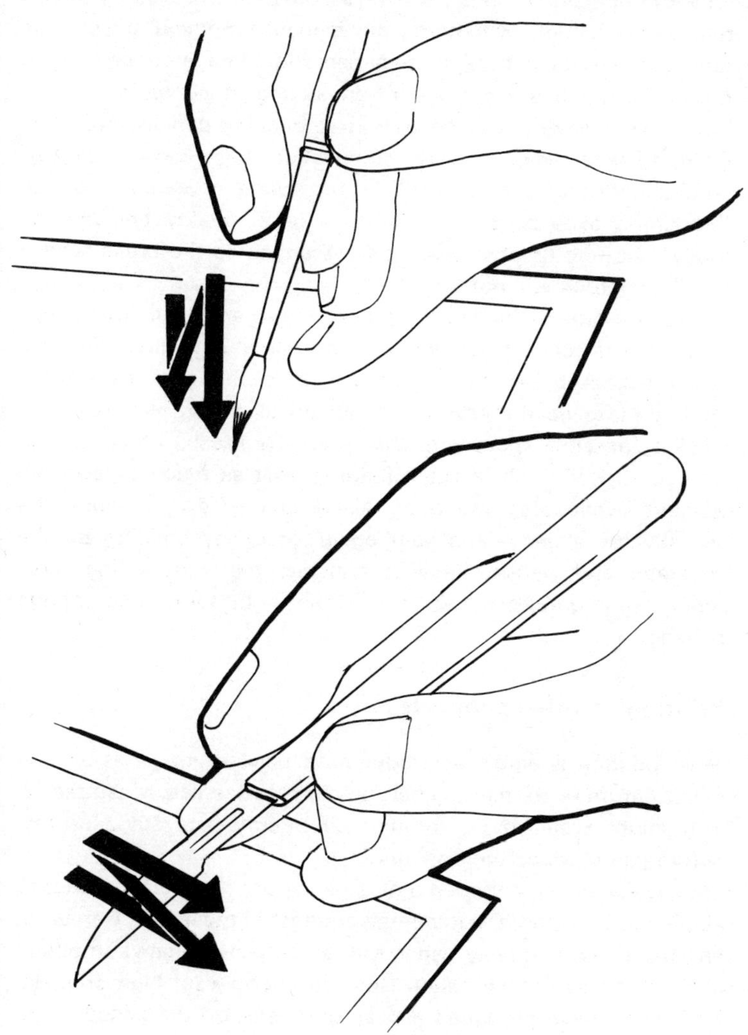

Hold the spotting brush almost vertically and use a stippling action to obliterate white spots or lines. Do not try to paint, and use the brush as dry as possible. Use the retouching knife very gently to scrape off black marks. Raise the blade between strokes.
Work slowly and patiently in both cases, building up the effect.

with the lightest of pressure with a corner of the blade you can remove black marks with hardly any evidence. Some of the gloss is removed from the paper (glossy papers should be retouched before glazing) but that is only evident from an angled viewpoint.

White marks have to be treated with retouching pencils, dyes, etc. Ordinary lead pencil is very effective on some paper surfaces, particularly semi- or dead matt, but the normal procedure is to use retouching dyes or pigments with a good quality fine-pointed brush. The fine point is absolutely essential, so the brush from a child's paintbox will not do.

Take a very little of the dye or pigment and spread it very thinly on a paper, china, plastic etc. surface and allow it to dry. With the brush almost bone dry–a gentle lick is the best moistening method–take up the absolute minimum of colour and make the smallest possible spots with the tip of the brush, which is held almost vertically. Fill in the offending spot as much as possible without overlapping the dots. Allow that to dry–it should be virtually dry already–and start again, gradually building up the coverage and density until it matches the surrounding area. Again, your greatest asset is a feather-light touch and infinite patience.

Printing on other supports

Most printing is aimed at producing a positive image as an end result but there are many other jobs that your enlarger can tackle. You might want to go through an intermediate stage or two before you produce the final print.

We have already mentioned that paper comes in different grades to allow you to increase or lower the contrast of the image. Generally, you use a less contrasty paper with a contrasty negative to obtain a more or less normal result. But you might want high contrast. You might have produced a near silhouette on the negative. To turn it into a complete silhouette, you print it on the hardest paper available.

Sometimes that is not enough. It is better to make another more contrasty negative and print from that. Nothing could be simpler. You can use your enlarger to print on film just as easily as on paper—or nearly as easily if you are working in 35 mm. As you want a silhouette, you use contrasty film and it is quite easy to obtain sheets of such film, known as line or lith film, in various sizes. Get the blue-sensitive type if you can because that can be used in ordinary safelighting, just like bromide paper. It can be processed perfectly satisfactorily in the same chemicals, too, but you get high contrast quicker if you use the recommended developer.

If your enlarger takes both 35 mm and 6 × 6 cm, it is reasonably easy to print on to the larger format and use the final high-contrast negative for enlarging in the normal way. If you can handle only 35 mm, it might be better to print on to film the same size as your final print so that you can contact-print the final result. We dealt with that when discussing proof printers.

Your first print from the negative on to line film is a transparency (positive image) that has to be printed again to produce a negative. This second printing should give all the contrast you require but you can repeat the process as often as you like.

Apart from high-contrast film, you can print on to ordinary film to produce a well-grade positive transparency of any required size. You can use sheet film in any of the well-known brands or specialized materials such as photo-linen and opal film (see the chapter on print-making materials). You can even buy emulsion to coat on to a variety of supports and another special type for firing on to ceramics. Both are expensive, the latter very expensive and available only to order. It also needs specialized equipment.

There are innumerable experimental processes that you can use in your darkroom, such as the production of poster-like prints, bas-relief images, solarizations and so on. These are beyond the scope of this book but you can find plenty of inspiration in another book in the series—Gunther Spitzing's *Focalguide to Enlarging* as well as many other books devoted to more advanced print-making methods.

Testing the safelight

The one essential for good darkroom work is an efficient safelight. It should give you plenty of light to work by but must be absolutely safe, ie, it must have no effect at all on your light-sensitive materials. If you are tempted to improvise your own safelight, you must test it. It is even wise to test any commercial product you use, if only for your own peace of mind.

That is not as simple a procedure as it might seem to be. The obvious way is to place a piece of bromide paper on the enlarger baseboard and obscure part of it with a coin or any other small opaque object. After a few minutes, develop the paper and if there is no trace of where the coin stood, your safelight is safe.

That is a rather rough and ready test that tells you little if anything. When you make a print, you do not only expose the paper to the safelight. You also use the light from the enlarger lamp. It is possible for the safelight to have no visible effect by itself but to put just enough light on the paper to overcome the inertia of the emulsion. It then needs only a fractional exposure from the enlarger lamp to produce a tone that the safelight alone would not have produced. The result is a slight veiling of the highlights and a merging of mid-tones that would otherwise be distinct and separate. If the fault is slight, you may not notice it but you will never get prints quite as good as they should be.

The best method of testing, therefore, is to place the coin on the paper as before but then, after a few minutes exposure to the safelight, to remove the coin and give a quick flash of light from the enlarger lamp (with no negative in the carrier) before processing the paper. If there is then no trace of where the coin stood, you can be satisfied with your safelighting.

The flash from the enlarger beam should be just sufficient to provide a visible tone on the paper after development, so you may need to experiment to find that exposure first. After your test, that tone should be unbroken across the paper. If your safelight is affecting the paper, the place where the coin stood will show up lighter because it did not receive the safelight exposure.

Alternatively, after the test exposure, make a print on the paper in the normal way. Again, there should be no trace of where the coin stood.

Printing in Colour

It might seem a little ambitious to talk of colour printing in such a basic book as this, but it is not. Colour processing has become a great deal easier in recent years and is now well within the scope of any darkroom worker. It is also a totally different process so that there is no reason why anybody should not start straight in on colour working without any grounding in black-and-white. On the other hand, it would be a pity if he were to stick to colour only, because black-and-white photography still has a definite niche of its own.

Compared with black-and-white, colour printing is expensive. It calls for a costly set of filters, special three-layer papers, and chemicals that cost a lot more than black-and-white developer and fixer. Moreover, the generally-accepted method of processing for the small user is the colour processing drum, which takes only small amounts of solution but dumps them after each use. The cost still compares favourably with commercial prints (when you get past the wastage stage) and the results may well be more to your liking, but you can still spend a lot of money on materials.

Negative/positive principles

The basic principles of colour printing from negatives are a little difficult to grasp at first. Not that you need to understand them fully to produce perfectly satisfactory prints. The following notes are for those who like to know where the nuts and bolts go. Your colour negative film has three light-sensitive layers—sensitive, from top to bottom, to blue, green and red light. These layers do not, however, form dyes of blue green and red. They form yellow, magenta and cyan respectively—the complementaries of blue, green and red. Yellow is red plus green (in light, not pigment), the complementary to blue. Magenta is red plus blue and complementary to green. Cyan is blue plus green, the complementary to red. In other words, the complementary of each primary is a mixture of the other two colours.

Thus, your colour negative has reversed tones and complementary colours, which are more suitable than the primaries for colour photography because they each pass two colours and block (or absorb) one. The paper on which you print the negative is similarly constructed but sometimes with the layers reversed. When you print through the cyan dye, which is in the red-sensitive layer of the film, it acts on both blue and green layers in the paper. As in the film, these layers form yellow and magenta dyes. To the eye viewing the print, a superimposition of transparent yellow and magenta dyes appears red. Thus, a red object forms a cyan image in the negative that is transformed into two images, yellow and magenta, in the print and the eye sees those images as red.

Few colours are pure, of course, and there may well be a weaker yellow or magenta image in the negative, too, producing magenta plus cyan or yellow plus cyan in the print to make the red less pure.

The dyes are formed in the negative by a special colour-forming developer which produces both the usual silver image (which is subsequently bleached out) and dye images in proportion to the silver deposits. Where the subject is white, heavy silver deposits and correspondingly dense dyes are produced in all three layers of the negative. Together, the three dyes filter out virtually all light from the enlarger lamp so that none gets through to form dyes in the paper. A black subject forms no dye image in the film but all three in the paper.

Colours that are mixtures of the primaries form dyes in more than one layer. Yellow, for example, produces cyan and magenta images in the red and green sensitive layers of the film. The cyan blocks red from the enlarger lamp and magenta blocks green, so only blue light is transmitted to form yellow dye in the blue sensitive layer of the paper.

The dyes used are not perfect because nobody has yet discovered perfect dyes for this purpose. The yellow dye, for example, cannot block off all the blue light, so some of it gets through to the other layers. To combat this and similar problems with the other dyes, there is a variable masking principle built into most colour negatives.

So the complementary-coloured negative image is overlaid by a strong orange or brown colour that almost obscures all other colours. The quality of a colour negative is therefore very difficult to judge by eye.

All this may seem difficult to follow at first but it has a perfectly logical basis and is worth reading through a couple of times. If you understand the principles, you are better able to deal with the difficulties of filtration.

Colour printing filters

The most satisfactory colour printing method is the so-called white-light or subtractive method. That is the only method we shall deal with here. An additive method, as we mentioned when dealing with enlargers, is also possible and can give perfectly good results, but it is troublesome in many ways and is best ignored by beginners despite the lower cost of the three filters.

Filters for the subtractive method are generally supplied as 7 × 7 cm sheets of coloured acetate film for negatives up to 6 × 6 cm. They are placed in a filter drawer in the enlarger where they alter the colour of the light passing through the lens, but have no effect on image quality. They come in a set of 17 or more, including a UV filter to absorb any unwanted ultra-violet radiation that might be emitted by the enlarger lamp. The rest are yellow, magenta and cyan in various densities expressed by two figures from, say, .025 to .99. The decimal point is usually omitted.

It is best to remember the filter colours in this order (think of YMCA) because filtration is commonly noted in the order yellow, magenta and cyan. The figures 50 30 00, for example, mean 50 yellow, 30 magenta and nil cyan.

The purpose of colour printing filters is to adjust the colour rendering of the negative and the colour quality of the light source to suit the characteristics of the paper. The dyes used in film and paper are not perfect and nor are those of the filters, so a certain amount of juggling is necessary to balance the one against the other to produce the best possible rendering of the original subject. This is a tricky process and can be extremely frustrating at first. With luck, however, we may be able to ease the path just a little.

Most part-time colour workers use acetate filters in a colour drawer but there are relatively expensive colour enlargers that have filters built in, controlled by dials or sliders on the lamphouse. The principle is exactly the same. It is just the practice that is a little easier. Instead of exchanging filters in the drawer, you simply turn a wheel or slide a knob along a scale. Some of these enlargers have special dyeless filters that work by interference, like the colours you see in an oil film on water. They are generally more stable than the dyed type and are not prone to fading with age.

You start colour printing in exactly the same way as black-and-white. You put the negative (or slide–we shall come to that later) in the carrier and project the image on the baseboard. Then, however, you have an additional step. You have to decide not only what exposure to give but what filtration to use. Variations from batch to batch of film and paper are such that you can never print without some filtration.

There are all sorts of instruments to help you through this stage but they all have to be calibrated from a perfect print before you can use them. So your first print has to be without instruments or other aids. Moreover this is a reference print to help you with all subsequent prints from the same type of film on the same type of paper. It has to be the best print you can possibly make.

You must choose a good clean negative with a reasonable range of normal colours–normal to you that is. If you take mostly portraits, your reference negative must have good skin tones. If you are a landscape type, you want normal daylit browns and greens, etc. Do not make your first print from a sunset, contra-jour, low-light or similar subject unless, of course, most of your work is in that field. Preferably this negative is one from which a good commercial print has already been made, because you cannot judge the negative yourself.

Test print for exposure

The only way to proceed now is by trial and error but you need a lot more paper than the 50 cm strip that suffices for black-and-white. Set your enlarger to the size of paper you are using and insert the filter pack recommended by the paper manufacturer, including the UV filter generally advised. On the outside of each pack of paper you will usually find a series of figures such as 70 40 00, which you will now be able to recognize as 70 yellow, 40 magenta and nil cyan. These figures change with each batch of paper and give you a baseline to work from and a comparison between one batch and another.

With your filters in place, compose and focus the image sharply on the baseboard and stop the lens down to about *f*8 or two or three stops from maximum aperture. Turn out all lights: you have to work in complete darkness. Position the colour paper on the baseboard (a masking frame is almost essential) and switch on the enlarger lamp. Set the timer, if you are using one, to 40 seconds. After five seconds, move a piece of black card or similar substance into the beam to obscure about a quarter of the image. After ten seconds, obscure one half, after 20 seconds three quarters and at 40 seconds, switch off the enlarger lamp.

It is a very good idea to run through this procedure with no paper on the baseboard because working in the dark is more than a little difficult until you get used to it. You could get set up, for example, start to move your black card into the light beam, only to realize that you cannot now see the clock. You need a method of timing in the dark. If you have a luminous sweep second hand or a metronome or whatever, you have no problem. Otherwise, try counting seconds on to a tape recorder and playing it back in the darkroom. Other ideas may occur to you in your particular situation. Your timing does not even have to be in seconds. It can be any reliably regular beat but seconds are advisable if you keep records. You might change your system at some later date. You should keep careful records, incidentally, of both time and filtration, not only because you might need to repeat a print, but because they offer some guidance for similar subjects in the future.

This test is for exposure only. Process the paper (we shall come to that later) and decide which strip shows the correct density, ignoring the colour. It should have detail in both highlight and shadow areas, except, of course, in the small unimportant extremes. You may have to make another test with a narrower range of exposures. Take care to get it right because this is an important print.

Assessing the colour cast

Having decided on the exposure, make a note of it. Now look at the colour of the strip. It will show a cast, perhaps to the extent of appearing to be one colour only. The problem now is to decide exactly what that cast is. Is it red or red-blue (magenta), blue or blue-green (cyan) and so on. It is likely, in fact, to be yellow, red or magenta. Having decided on the predominant colour of the cast, you have to adjust the basic filter pack in the enlarger drawer. Assume that the cast is magenta, ie, there is too much magenta in the image. We have shown that the magenta dye is formed in the green-sensitive layer of the paper, so to reduce the amount of magenta dye formed, we have to reduce the amount of green light reaching the paper. The filter that absorbs green light is magenta so, strangely, in colour negative work, you always add filters of the colour of the cast. The same effect is obtained, of course, by reducing filtration in the other two colours. You must not have all three coloured filters in the pack together because equal densities of all three colours simply add up to a neutral density that does nothing more than reduce the intensity of the light without affecting its colour. So, if you had a basic filtration of 70 00 20, you would not add 20 magenta to make 70 20 20. You would take out the equal densities from the other two colours–20 00 20– and adjust the filter pack to 50 00 00.

To return to our example, we have a basic filter pack of 70 40 00 and have decided that we have a magenta cast. We now have to decide how strong the cast is and how much filtration it requires to remove it. If you can see other colours in the print, the cast is probably no more than about 20–30. It is best to move slowly, so add 20 magenta and make your pack 70 60 00. That indicates a heavyish cast but with other colours discernible. If the other colours are quite clear but somewhat overlaid with magenta, add no more than 10 magenta.

We have decided to add 20 magenta but we are not finished yet because we have added density to the filter pack and that means less light getting through to the paper from the enlarger lamp. There should be a table with your filters to indicate what effect each has on exposure. This is usually expressed by a filter factor, by which you have to multiply the originally-estimated exposure— or divide, if you have subtracted filters. A 20 magenta filter is likely to have a factor of about 1.2, so you have to multiply the exposure of which you made a note, say 15 seconds, by 1.2, which gives 18. So, at last, you arrive at settings for a trial print—a filter pack of 70 60 00, and exposure of 18 seconds at *f*8. You can now make a print on that basis. If you have judged the cast correctly, you are home and dry. If you did not, and that is much more likely, you have to examine the new print, assess its cast and try again.

At this stage you should at least have recognizable colours in your print, so you can try assessing the filtration needed by viewing the print through your colour printing filters. Take filters that you think are opposite in colour to the cast ie, cyan and yellow for a magenta cast, and pass them fairly rapidly in front of the print about half way between your eyes and the print. Do not stare through them: try to make up your mind quickly. When the print looks right, add filtration of half the value of the viewing filters and of the complementary colour. You may decide, for example, that your print looks right through 20C and 20Y filters. For that, you add 10M.

There is no short cut to producing your first print. You just have to keep at it until you get it right. But you must start with a good negative and that is why it is best to use one from which you have already seen a good print. You know then that it can be printed correctly and you have something with which to compare your results. Have patience and keep on until you are sure you have the best possible print. Then you can go ahead and print from any similar subject on the same film stock and the same batch of paper with the same filtration. You may still need slight changes for different subjects or different batches of paper but you have a good basis to work from.

When you buy another batch of paper, the filtration will almost certainly change because there will be a different basic filter pack recommendation on the packet. Whereas your first packet may say 70 40 00, the next may recommend 75 25 00. If your negatives required you to alter the filtration for the first batch to 70 60 00, you must vary the pack for the second batch in the same way, by adding 20 magenta, so the filtration becomes 75 45 00.

If you print on the same paper but from another type of film, it is likely that the filtration will change radically and you will have to make another reference print for those circumstances. Similarly, different types of picture in different lighting may need alterations in the filter pack and, if you make many pictures of that type, you should have a reference negative for that too. Keep careful notes of all these reference negatives and prints, with exposure time for print size (or magnification, or enlarger head height), filter pack and any other points you think worthy of note. If you eventually get round to buying a colour analyser, you will need all the reference negatives you can find because they work on the principle of analysing a particular shade of colour (skin tone, neutral grey, etc.) and you need areas of similar colour and brightness in each negative, or at least in one of a batch taken at the same time. That is why some photographers like to include a standard grey card in one of their shots, just out of the picture, to be used for colour analysis.

Printing from slides

The negative-positive process is not the only method of colour printing. It is also possible to make colour prints direct from slides—by reversal processing or by a dye-destruction process.

Reversal processing depends on two development steps—the first to produce a negative silver image in the usual way, the second to produce a positive silver image from the halides unaffected by the original exposure. That can be done in black-and-white or colour but in colour, of course, a dye image is produced with the second silver image. This is the method used for processing colour slides.

An essential of this method is that the halides unaffected by the original exposure are fogged after the first development to make them developable. The fogging may be by re-exposure to light or by chemical action.

After fogging, the positive image is developable by a colour developer that also releases dyes in the emulsion, while the negative image, having already been developed, can form no dye. The film is a tripack (three light-sensitive layers) just like the negative and works in exactly the same way, using yellow, magenta and cyan dyes. In the reversal film, however, because it is the layers not affected by the camera exposure that produce the dyes, a red subject produces yellow and magenta dyes in the blue and green sensitive layers. To the viewer, yellow and magenta make red.

Similarly, green grass produces dye in the blue and red sensitive layers of yellow and cyan, which look green to the viewer. A black subject has no direct effect on any of the layers so all produce dyes, combining to look black to the viewer.

Printing from the slide so produced is basically the same process. The yellow and magenta dyes forming the red object absorb blue and green from the enlarger lamp and allow only the red-sensitive layer of the paper to be affected. The first development prevents the light-affected parts from being subsequently developed by the colour developer which therefore acts only on the corresponding area in the blue and green sensitive layers to produce yellow and magenta dye images. These images again combine to form a red image to the eye. In both cases, of course, film and print, the silver images are bleached out to leave only the dye images.

The dye-destruction process arrives at the same result by a different route. The paper in this case (plastic actually) contains dyes in all three layers and looks virtually black when unexposed. Exposure makes the dyes susceptible to colour development but development in this case destroys the dyes instead of creating them. Thus, only the red sensitive layer is affected by light from a red part of the slide. That layer contains cyan dye which is therefore destroyed on development, leaving yellow and magenta dye images in the other two layers to present a red image to the eye. A transparent part of the slide, representing white, exposes all layers and the developer destroys all dyes, leaving the paper white.

This process has the advantage that it is simpler to understand. Filtration seems to be more logical to those who do not fully understand the principles of the neg-pos process. A cast is removed by subtracting filters of the same colour as the cast. The dyes used are said to be more satisfactory and less subject to fading. Certainly the process is easier to handle, with relatively low-temperature working and considerable latitude in both time and temperature.

On the other hand, of course, for those accustomed to printing from negatives, it seems a little strange in both the normal reversal and dye-destruction processes that overexposure leads to a print that is too light.

Colour print processing

The most popular method of colour print processing for the part-time user is by processing drum. The reason is obvious: there is nothing else in his price range. The drum wins by default, although it is a cumbersome piece of equipment with many drawbacks. You can use open trays or dishes as in black-and-white work (or even the special type of covered dish if it is still available) but that entails a certain amount of paddling about in the solutions in total darkness, which is just not on for most people.

We mentioned when describing the available equipment, a colour box that is virtually nothing more than a plastic box with deep containers in which you dip double-sided print holders. It has an enormous capacity and is very easy to handle in the dark but it has a price tag that, although lower than most other processors, makes it more suitable for those who intend to print commercially. It has refinements such as a heater for a capacious water jacket, inlet and outlet for a washing tank and so on but the small user could improvise in those areas if he had the tanks and the paper holders. We must emphasize, incidentally, that whenever we mention cost, we are referring largely to the UK market. In some countries these items may well be less expensive.

So, unless you can fork out a considerable sum of money, you are confined to the efficient (it certainly works very well) but time-consuming processing drum. Fortunately, you can now process most papers with just two or three solutions.

The drum is virtually a plastic pipe, (one, at least, is made from a section of commercial drain-pipe) sealed at one end and light trapped at the other in various ways to allow solutions to be poured in and out. One version has to be stood up while solutions are poured in, to be stored in a container until the drum is returned to the horizontal. Another has an elongated pouring lip to allow solutions to be poured in with the drum in a horizontal position.

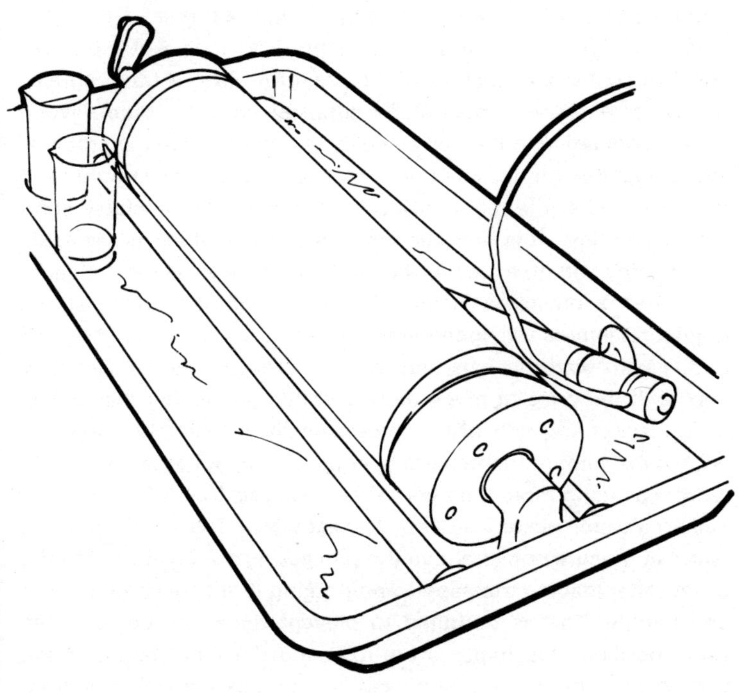

A simple method of temperature control for colour printing. A gravel tray forms a water jacket with a submersible heater adapted for photography. The processing drum is mounted in the tray and flasks of solutions are also placed in the water to keep them at the required temperature.

All drums use small amounts of solution, say 50 ml for a 20 × 25 cm (8 × 10 inch) print and rely on constant agitation, which can be a bit wearing. The agitation should be in two dimensions to avoid streaky results and various methods are used to provide that. One drum has a handle at one end and a slot engaging a peg in a stand at the other to provide both end-to-end and round-and-round sloshing of the solutions as the handle is turned.

This is, in fact, a useful version to be used in a water bath to stabilize solution temperatures. The faithful old grit tray contains the water and the special stand supplied with the drum. Warm water is poured in to the tray at a degree or two above the processing temperature and, except in the coldest conditions should keep the solutions at the required level throughout the relatively short processing time. It is only the developer temperature that is really critical. You can go a step further and introduce a thermostatically-controlled submersible heater that will keep the water at the required temperature indefinitely. There are various commercial outfits with water jackets and even motorised agitation but they approach the price of much more versatile processing machinery. If you are stuck with drum processing, it is better to improvise your own form of temperature control and agitation. It is not worth spending more than you have to on this form of processing. Failing a water jacket, you use pre-heat water. This entails pouring water at a degree or so above the processing temperature into the drum (after loading the paper) and pouring it out again after about one minute. That is designed to prevent the much cooler drum (and, possibly, the paper) from lowering the temperature of the very small amount of solution used. If your darkroom and the drum are already at the processing temperature (possible with the dye-destruction process) the pre-heat should not be necessary. On the other hand, in such circumstances, you should be storing the paper in a refrigerator or at least in a cool place and that alone could drop the developer temperature.

Loading the paper in to the drum is a simple enough process if you are not too ambitious. Each drum has its own method but the basic idea is that the paper is put in with the emulsion toward the centre of the drum and the back on the drum wall, where it sticks as the drum rotates. The drums are generally designed to take one 8 × 10 inch or 11 × 14 inch sheet but may have a divider to allow a number of smaller prints to be inserted. The difficulty in some designs arises when you attempt to insert more than two. There is no reliable way of preventing one riding over another.

With the drum loaded and the lid replaced, you pour in the specified amount of developer, which has previously been brought up to the working temperature. (If you are not using a water jacket, you pour pre-heat water in and out before the developer.) Note the time the developer goes in exactly. You must stick strictly to the time and temperature instructions. Pour the developer out at the end of the specified time and drain the drum as much as possible. The rest of the solutions then follow according to the manufacturer's instructions but the time is not so important for solutions other than the developer. You must not bleach or fix normal dye-forming processes for less than the specified time but these operations are taken to finality so excess time is of no importance. In fact, in case the solution temperature has dropped a little it does no harm to let the bleach and fix run a little over time. Processing temperatures are generally rather high—from 27-38°C (80-100°F). When a rinse is needed between solutions, that has to be at the same temperature and meanwhile you have to keep the other solutions warm, too. In a cold darkroom without running hot water that can be tiresome. A picnic stove could come in very useful, but the best answer is really a thermostatically-controlled water jacket for the drum, and small flasks or measures containing the processing solutions.

The small quantities of solutions used in processing drums make storage in small containers a practical proposition. After making up the developer, for example, you can decant it into a dozen or more 100 ml plastic bottles filled to the stopper. If you use only half of the quantity each time, you can squeeze the bottle to expel air. Unused developer will keep for many weeks in this way. There is no need to break the other solutions up because they do not deteriorate so rapidly.

Despite the care needed with colour prints and the lack of really suitable equipment for the small user, colour print processing is now almost as simple as black-and-white—in the mechanical sense. It still needs experience, skill, perhaps even flair in the exposure and filtration stages but processing has been reduced to a reasonably straightforward time and temperature process. If it were not for the need to work in total darkness, there would be nothing to it. If only some manufacturer could come up with some simple, reasonably-priced processor with a better capacity than the drums and using an economical solution-replenishment system, it would be about as easy as it could get. There is a real gap here between the drum and more ambitious systems that are really designed for almost constant use. The trouble seems to lie with the equipment manufacturers, as it did with the film manufacturers a few years ago. They underestimate the ability and ingenuity of the so-called amateur photographer and try to provide him with the foolproof equipment that may well be needed for production-line working.

Index